Borderlines

An Astral Experience in Poems

Alan Botsford

For Minako

Also by Alan Botsford

Poetry

mamaist: New and selected poems

Dreamer: Poems in Culture

Possessions: Poems in American Poetry

mamaist: a different sort of light

A Book of Shadows (with William I. Elliott)

mamaist: learning a new language

Hybrid

Walt Whitman of Cosmic Folklore: Dialogues, Essays, Poems
for Reimagining Walt Whitman in the 21st Century

Contents

Foreword

I

It's true—in finding the words,
you find the world underway.
But what happens when what
happened is a thing one cannot say,
where what is lost is loss itself
reenacted in the quotidian fray?

In these poems, an amalgam of voices
that took shape over many years, is offered
a glimpse of being a foreigner in Japan, a life
for all its limitations that has been richly
rewarding in being empoeticized, as it were,
in its struggle to avoid cliches of 'Zen Japan'
and bringing into balance energies both east and west.

I have not wished to titillate or to thrill;
so far as I can manage it, this is history,
and (again as far as I can manage it), accurate history.

Give me prestige and power with which to canoodle
with the stars, and I'll give you greatness
bargained for that imagination and connection,
in full swing, lament they ever bore witness.

From masks to personas to brands,
the human self is always evolving.
My story? Hearing it is a story in itself.

If there is ancestral wisdom to be found,
it is in telepathy setting the agenda.

It's a miracle you're here
It's a miracle you're there
Everywhere's too small a word
for the things I've heard.

Running day and night, collisions
at energies never seen before take place.

What this is
is cosmic nature.

You don't know anything about it?
What you don't know anything about, keeps you alive.

I would suggest anyone reading this to take heed:
it is not for the faint-hearted nor thin-skinned.

Adam in a sea of voices heard God
say it was time and so he rhymed
his way to the beginning again where
it all had started in the garden long ago,
to babble up a tower he climbed
following the sun he would know
along narrow streets of Babylon.

In this complex symbiosis of self and others
is formed a secret autobiography,
self-portraits out of others, if you will.

Recorder, did you think you wrote

by yourself? You have co-authors
who help you write the book
of your life, without whom page
after page would be blank.

The muse of me
is the muse of us.

All they are are actors,
their speech in calamity otherwise,
he notes, himself on a stage.

Portrait of myself
  as others.

In dreams, I am not
other people, but
other people are me.

I became the ghostwriter of my own life.
But the question is,
when the ghost writes, am I
plagarizing others real or imaginary?

None of this is true; it is all true.

For how long have I been wrong
until I was finally right
where I belong…

To inside
what is soul.

II

"Competition, we know, forms the engine of modern life.
And poetry is often about, and limited by, one's poetic persona.
These poems, however, originating as they do in dream states,
proffer a more collaborative view. What Botsford's after
in these channeled poems, he says, is post-persona, poetry
behind or beneath the façade propping up the otherwise
indestructible edifice of the self as property to be defended.
Here is found no mistrust of the unassimilable other.
When you have the energies of your personality
being channeled into poetry, you no longer have
a personality as we ordinarily define it; it is more
like Keats' poet as mutable chameleon, or Eliot's
continual extinction of self.

"The top guns, the heavy hitters, the big wigs,
they know how to use language to preserve
and consolidate their power. Don't expect
much exploratory action from them, lest
they risk losing what they have worked
hard to establish—a foothold in the pantheon
of the culture. This trance poet, on the contrary,
has gone where the flow of interchange has
taken him, each poem for him a questioning,
a listening and, whenever possible, a discovery."

    These poems came into being in Japan.
    Indeed, it could be said that Japan brought
    these poems into being through me.

"Not one conscious thought, he says, went
into the making of many of these poems.

The poems happened as written.
Which raises the question: how
did the poems come about?
Where do they come from, he asks.
How did they just write themselves?
If it's not death of the author, where has the author gone?
If he's given these sentences then are they his?
If these words aren't his, then whose are they?
Indeed in what sense were the voices
ever 'his' to begin with? How, in other
words, could he have conversations without,
in a way, being there? How is it that he had
opened himself up to voices he had no
control over, and in which he could
take little proprietory interest?"

    When you open yourself with pen in hand,
     you open up the radio transmitter and take in
     all sorts of things…voices flow through you,
     so many voices coming in over the airwaves.

    These poems register influxes of energy,
    influences, if you will.
    Certain figures called out to me,
     as Roethke would say, that is, they
    absorbed me, or assimilated me, not
     the other way around. I take this to be
    a poet's way of entering into
    the dance of influence.

    The channeled poetry in which I take little proprietary
     interest haunts me regardless. They aren't my words
     yet they come from my hand, since it is I who write them.

Merrill's strategy of 'quoting' spirits from séances
at the Ouija board seems ingenious to me now.

The voice I had stumbled upon
had the inflections of a multitude
of different voices. (Writing outside
your own identity is not a stretch
when you don't have an identity
to speak of, that is, again, when you, like Keats's
chameleon poet, inhabit multiple identities.)

While recording whatever I picked up in
those psychic frequencies of the hive mind,
or my unconscious mind, I caught the speech
rhythms of everyday life which took shape
in the natural compression of the poem.

The aim is not to become a mouthpiece for others
who already have a voice, but rather to filter through
the imagination some of the voices of our time as a
homage created directly from my lived experience
of them, and to breathe another's breath in the bargain
(the devil's) in an act of deep empathy.

"Thoughts and prayers, we send others
in their hour of need. Do we know
what it means to hear thoughts and prayers
coming in over the transom of our consciousness,
affecting our otherwise inviolable minds?
For the creative act, nothing is more powerful
than the subconscious. From it springs creation."

Will some of these inciendary poems rankle the poets?

"You're the Davy Crockett of this frontier, have no fear!
That's the burden of being a pioneer—
always having to backtrack for others.
Everyone can work to remix and
reimagine their world."

    Close to thirty years a homeland left
     to found between us what I thought
     was lost—you whom I dream of, eyes
     open, and you whom I wake for,
      closed. As far back as memory takes me
     as far forward as imagination allows,
      I travel east and west with my heart
     rooted in the image of this freedom
     I've never fully known, nor
      will ever take for granted.

"The self, he reminds us,
is composed, like music,
of different registers and different
chords and different notes.

"Outlaw?
The law
of mystery
was the law he obeyed.

"From the outside the whole thing looks mad,
but from the inside it all makes perfect sense.

"'The real inside story never was told before.
No one could possibly tell it until now and stay alive.'
from *The Naked Street*"

There was no wisdom of the east to which I subscribed,
unless it was wisdom of the weast, whatever that was,
that I had been living for most of my adult life in Japan,
speaking a Japanese predicated on my American identity,
and writing an English predicated on my Japanese.
So where had I arrived, then, in my killing the Buddha?

I

'I set out to record the existence'

I set out to record the existence,
as I experienced it, of the invisible
world, the spirit world, the energy
world, not to prove its superiority
over the objective visible world
(impossible) but to affirm the balance
of forces both known and unknown
that contribute to the formation
of the human experience of our world.

The poet's imaginative reconstruction
of his inner environment does not
make him immune to struggles for
power that take place all around him.

If these were songlines to reorient yourself by,
be prepared to live along ghostly demarcations
in that 'hell under the skull-bones.'

A song of the open road of continuous
interactions, reactions and transactions.

Exchanges are memorable ones that rearrange experience
to a newer state, now of chaos, now of grace, that evince
the fate we call our own, where none else will convince.

I went through this, mine
from beginning to end, the line
of thought leading to experience

in the physical sphere, whose influence
upon the mental sphere doubled back
on itself and reconstituted as luck.

When each of us is clearly 'someone to know,'
who, then, gets the hearing they deserve?
Who will have his or her say and be heard?
Democratic politics, as messy as it gets, wades
in deep to guarantee the right to be heard.
Which is, in effect, the right to vote and to have it count.
Is this no different from the fictional imagination
at work, in giving voice to one's imagined others?

What is outside
the exile if
not the world
he's inside of,
that he longs
to remake inside
himself.
        How much,
then, leave out?
How much cleave
to the view
he finds?

Recognition from our peers, or superiors,
makes what's posterior, anterior, and conjoins
to make us less afraid of our interior.

Don't keep your secrets to yourself
when it's time for show and tell.
No matter what hell there is to pay,
however, don't sell yourself short.

The spillway of the mind's
release into the vagaries of
thought, is a river stepped
into with no escape from itself,
its current taking you along
for the ride.

Where the subject matter is reception,
the challenge is to keep one's roots alive and well.

My older brother jokes I'd be happy
living under a tree anywhere
in the world. He's not altogether wrong.

Mining the heart
that arts the mind,
I never know
what I
—magpie of
the cosmic I—
will find.

What I heard them say is not
what they said per se. But I
can't get what they said out
of my head, so here they are,
the voices I've heard, words
verbatim spoken to and through
me, found accidentally.

No, I'm not going to describe it for you
from the outside, I want you to
experience it from the inside…

'A bluish Whitman' (*from* Meta Frenz)

(their voices)

"He's a bluish Whitman."

"Says who?"

"Says me, he says."

"What shall we say?"

"Say nothing and wait."

"Our minister has a dark side."

"The side that's dark makes his art."

"You're right. What's left?"

"Everything. Wait and see."

"Splashdown the rocket booster.
The sea is an open vault of human filth and misery."

"It's not of his making, he's sure of that."

"He's gone too far."

"He's not gone far enough."

"He's gone…"

"Don't count on it. He'll be back."

"What makes you think so?"

"Because we're his captive audience.
The steps he's dancing are being made up
as he goes along. It's all new territory for him."

"You mean, he's walking across the abyss without a net?"

"That's right. What's more, he knows we know."

"So why does he do it?"

"Because he has nowhere else to go except towards
the unknown. He knew what he was in for when
he began long ago."

"It's astonishing. I've never seen anything like it."

"Neither have I. We'll likely not see anything like
it again, either."

"What do you mean?"

"He is an avatar of some past literary great, possibly
sent by him or her to bear witness to/for us. This is
his life's work, doing what he's doing."

"How does he stand it?"

"He's an explorer. He's made for this.
It's his nature. Read his books, you'll see.
He's fresh, original, surprising, and yes never
a dull moment. It keeps him alive, his mission."

"What is he, some kind of knight? …Or nut?"

"Neither. He's more of a teacher who sings what
he has to teach, or a musician who sings to others his way."

"He was struck by a bolt of lightning?"

"Yeah. That's what he told me. He was forever
changed by it, he said. But he's shy about
talking about it openly. He has secrets."

"I like a man who has secrets. This plot grows
thicker every day!"

"He's not here to play. He's the real deal, mistakes
and all. He makes no excuses for himself."

"I'd say that's respectable."

"It's admirable, I agree. He's taking no short cuts.
What he is, is noble, sincere and profound. He's
no clown. He won't mess with us. That's not his
thing. He wants to sing, to try to bring something
to the world."

"Don't we all?"

"Not like him. He comes from pain and suffering with a message that gives him wings. For others, they might sink. But he flies."

"How does he manage?"

"I don't know. His wife and son have always been there for him, it's clear. He's not afraid as long as they're in the picture. His life is a team effort and he knows where to find his well of strength and that he can't go it alone. He's experimenting with his life, in ongoing collaboration. And it works for him. The poet-explorer-spaceman has learned lots of tricks along the way and he shares them all and still struggles. It's never easy for him."

"No drugs? No sex?"

"Apparently not."

"Who can live like that?"

"Evidently he can. And does. He's showing us how it can be done."

"But he's no saint!"

"Far from it. He has too much of a sense of humor and irony ever to take sainthood seriously."

"Still, why does he do it?"

"I say he wants people talking about him. He's not
some serial killer, he's a serial lover, of the platonic
kind. That's my take, anyway."

"What's a 'mamaist'?"

"Whatever it is, he's the prototype. Nobody's gone
before him. It has something to do with being
an empirical mystic, but I'm not sure. It's pretty cool.
And scientific. He's not into the bogeyman stuff.
He's more into language."

"I think he's got a hero complex."

"Maybe he does, but he uses that to his advantage.
He knows himself pretty well by now. He's aiming
to be unforgettable."

"A legend in his own mind?"

"And now, maybe, in ours too."

South Asian Restaurants

i

"Who is this *gaijin*, I see right through him.
I, dark-skinned, know a liar when I see one,
a whitey to boot, and I mean to kick
his ass. He dares come into my restaurant
as if he owned the space? A face of an angel,
no less. Some trace of Europe written all over
it, too. Would he speak English to me?
I'll teach him a thing or two in Bengali—
the skinny of a dirt-poor farmer come
to Japan to wear a mask."

ii

"What manner of man is this
who spins around in his bliss?
In aimless wandering, like us,
perhaps, hoping to make a sale
or have others hear his tale
the only way he can tell it,
or the only way he can sell it?
New to the block *we* are,
the neighborhood we'd hoped
might flock here, hasn't shown up yet,
but we've got stock and future shares
in where we'll be months from now.
Our *gaijin* customer throws his weight
lightly around, no *Nihongo* from his lips

but on English terms we all meet
today, to seal the deal not steal
the money from our karmic wheel."

Japanese Publisher

(his voice)

"Botsford has an eye
for women but he won't fly
the coop. He loves and cherishes
his wife, but oh the strife
he must have endured at the
hands of balling profs. Enough
I've seen of the world to know
the price he's paid, and continues
to pay. I'll throw him a lifeline
and play benign. It's the least
I can do for this American in Japan
who smiles in the bargain. A poet
without a name is a waif without
a home in my book. The world
won't read, let alone open,
his text of harmony and bliss,
and can you blame us? Ours
is a land riven by war. We
who whore for more life
suck dry as dirt the living heart.
Call us the undead. We have fed
on the likes of you for our bread.
It's nature's beast of the East, and
the rest the West will never know!"

American Poet (*from* Meta Frenz)

(his voice)

"A splendid line of language he's descended
from I can tell, I can feel it! And feel it well!
Buying the safest place in town has never been
more difficult. He bows to the idols we won't
worship—those of mystery, dreams, and irrationality
—or, properly speaking, Intuition, which, I'll say
for myself, I have an abundance of. Still, no power
or wealth accrues to it, so why set a tent up in his camp?
Besides, the woods I can't stand more than half a day in,
then it's back to sipping cognac and telling gay jokes
with friends. He has no inkling of my world, yet his
world is so much bigger and younger than mine,
and for that I won't forgive him.

"The images are personal, close, and downstairs.
We can visit, but how he lives that way is beyond
me and my limited powers of comprehension.
Still, a model showman of a psychical kind
we don't see too many of. He says nothing
outright of 'love' but that's what it takes, and
he knows costs mount for what he calls
the creative task. He's no Blakean that I can
see, by the way. He was yanking our chain
on that one, throwing a bone to history, too.
A Jungian perhaps, of the sidelong glancing
kind. It seems what's indispensable is
trance state and a pipeline to the subconscious

he won't speak openly about. Opening that
can of worms would only box him in, with
no hope of escape. I can't blame him there.
It's a rat's ass the world gives for it, and he
knows it, too. He'll keep playing chicken,
though, with his vehicles of thought and
whoever's coming down the pike…

"Chance of a lifetime he has seized, it looks like.
What price paid to his well-being we can glean
from his latest musings—quite high, I'd say.
Demons, he says, make my day! And they've
gotten the better of him nine times out of ten.
Time is telling us to stall, and we do. But him?
He's too tall for all of us small-timers. That
one in ten he wrestles out into the open
leads him into terrain gorgeous beyond belief…"

American Friend

(his voice)

i

"Alan has lost the compass to my heart
so I will give him my head's instead, writing
him today to tie the knot of *Not* the same,
Not one-world, *Not* Asian and *Not*, above
all, Japanese! We here in the U.S.A.—
where once upon a time you dwelled—
lift the individual up to the heights far
above the group impulse or instinct,
primitive we know it to be. For we
in the States—remember Walt?—value
gold dug up for real, a nugget at a time.
Deal-making, it's called, here in the world.
And everyone out here feels as I do—that
feelings followed fuzzily lose the path
of respect I fully intend to stay on—
the path hoisting the banner of I AM
above the field of WE ARE. For that's how
mankind is, how we advance, unsparing
of sentiment, unsettling of heart, doing
whatever it takes to come out! Ahoy!
To cast out half-baked half-breeds of
so-called East-West unions! What happened
to your life, Alan, as son of U.S.A.? You
essay into newer waters, only to be drowned
there, or half-drowned, like the rat you are.

After all, it's our shores you abandoned.
And the dot you became, as we in our boat
recede from your "farther shore," all but
vanishes from sight… No light you are
to my eye, certainly not to steer home by.
Why lie? You've moved down the totem
pole to stay "whole," yet are barely recognizable
to us anymore. Soul-space is no place for we
who live and die in the body. What made
you blink and think otherwise? Jesus rides
the milk train to Paradise, whether or not
Jew knew it. Besides, blond's fun is more
of the sun. Even the darkie in the White
House knows that, too. D.C. parades past
his front lawn to remind him who's really
Boss. It's a toss-up between Congress red
and Congress blue. Either way, we've sued
the pants off of you, and what do you have?
A cave you can crawl back into, to that human
inmost event of birth. Meanwhile, I'll breathe
death deep into my lungs and watch my breath,
exhaling, spread over earth in a gulp of success."

ii

"We travel the globe and glean
what we can of mysteries seen
and unseen that you're fond of,
Alan, but what have you got
to show for it, I ask you, all
of us tailgating the vehicle
in front leading the way, hogging
the lane, even, so that we can't

pass. Metaphors aside, you get
my drift. There's always the next
town to see, the next trip to take,
and we're lucky to get to go
and stay on the merry-go-round of
grandparenting and parenting,
enough for two lifetimes if
you ask me, and then some."

iii

"Alan you are nothing like I imagined you to be—
you are sweet, gentle, good-natured, a poet
who doesn't flaunt it, and a teacher to boot?
What's not to like? The careers of our sons
we follow like a bloodhound, the father's way,
while the politics of our time disheartens me
and threatens 250 glorious years of democracy.
Why hast thou forsaken us, I would ask God,
were I not a Jew with a vivid sense of history.
Time will tell what I cannot—where all this will
lead us. But sharing time and space with you
has been a treat, though you and Japan a mystery."

'Voyager into deep space' (*from* Meta Frenz)

(their voices)

"Errors are like your friends—
they pull you out of the
morass of perfection."

"Voyager into deep space
doesn't tell us where he's
going to next, he wanders
for the sake of a text".

"He hunkers down in
his new agenda.
May it take him far."

"I'll be alright then."

"Kindness will *not* keep
you afloat."

"The air will have been
let out of his tires."

"He never tires of
the element he's in."

Where's that?

"Air. It's what he's
made of, don't forget."

"He's no ham sandwich.
He's a lamb that
bleats for his breakfast."

"His open pen puts him in the lion's den.
He'll never get out alive.
Publishing his lines may be
a posthumous affair, 'cause he wouldn't
dare walk the line of the Other Side
on This Side. Or would he?
He'll carry a torch for his muse
right out of Eden, that's no lie.
Before he does it, I'd ask him why
put himself in harm's way all awry
as these poems would put him, testaments
of a bursting brain brimming with ideas
to die for, could we but live by them."

'Will you have seen me' (*from* Meta Frenz)

"These occult concoctions, as some might call them,
a journey—if you dare—into the cosmic mind…"

"Alan-san lowers the boom on banality
of evil, exploding the myth of the Western
self as that ruse of a subliminal muse
hungry for affirmation, needy for approval,
dying (and killing) for recognition, that one self at
the exclusion of all other selves, the one seeking
validation and proof of its inviolable existence as
the terminal point in a landscape of terminal
points, as an omniscient, phallocentric event
occurring in spacetime asynchronous with otherness,
a leaf in the reflecting pool of consciousness."

*

The drink, the cigarette, the porn pic
refused, just so, for confirmation
that one owns desire, not the other
way round, betrays a lack not of
imagination but of protocol: we'd
sack the citadel of power when
it's actually we powering the citadel
all the way to the home we'll never get to,
which is the point, isn't it, of refusal.
Desire otherwise placated is turf surrendered
in a war of attrition that nobody wins
and everybody loses his or her place

to the Other forever on the move
in a fluid mix within a borderless state
of ungovernable impulses. Hence the decline
in the value which the self depends on for itself,
if not, alas, for the Other it once was.

*

"You know, any loosening up of
the structure of the self, that monumental
edifice the West has built up over
centuries, is to the good, for the lessons
we can learn and implement in the
coming world we'll inhabit."

"Will you have seen me, will you have heard me
are, in so many words, the questions he no longer asks."

"No suburbs of the imagination for me, says he;
I aim for the City, tidal pulls notwithstanding."

"Power's edifice that constrains and imprisons
is nothing more or less than ego. But open the
channel where the creative flows and now you are free
to come and go. For we are made to flow creatively,
and the flow—even if dangerous—makes us
creative and helps us grow."

*

The heartland ink I write in
ventriloquizes its reception.

The weight lays its heaviness
upon my spirit and I take up
a pen to alleviate it—pressing
into its service all that my
imagination can muster.
The valves of spirit then open
and, as I step out of the way,
words flow forth. Here's where
voices from the depths reach
upwards and make themselves heard
to your ears as you who, taking dictation,
write it all down.

*

"East and West are reconfigured altogether.
Time to overhaul the paradigm communally!"

*

It's my story.
I must be kind
to my tension
and my release.
There's a vaster story
than the one
in the news
with each passing day
of violence and death.

Everybody in the know
is trying to grow
not for the Big Show

necessarily, although
that's the carrot on the stick. No,
it's something else, the trick
the mind plays on itself
for, call it redemption, or salvation,
or restoration, or absolute reparation
that will make one's life, seemingly, co-
here, whole.

*

"His poems suggest there are
technicians of grief
working behind the scenes."

"Germane to his project
is his disdain for rep."

"No, it's a smokescreen.
He's after bigger fish."

"One deep connection
behind the scenes of suffering."

"I'm just in awe
of its behavior."

"He's rejected both lives, East and West.
 It's a third way he's onto, exploring
 a path yet to appear to us clearly..."

"He questions the unquestionable
alliance between good and evil."

"Energies coursing through the environment
naturally will affect our lives on many levels."

"Sex is pretty routine.
That's what being an adult means
behind the everyday persona's screen."

"Who he's writing about we don't have,
because he doesn't exist."

Expatriate American Poet & Translator

(his voice)

i

"Anything he hears, he rearranges to
a new fluency, it appears, which runs
from darkness into the light where
consciousness shines bright. I wouldn't
put sorcery past him, but past all that
he says he is. He rather wants to
ring out the purposes of civilization,
or at least the mind we call civilized,
for a new view he says we're overdue.
I don't see Reason replaced any time
soon, having been our DNA this long.
Still and all, for a song without reason,
he rhymes soulfully, even at times
beautifully, and that's no mean feat.
Science in our day and age masters
the mysteries he'd have poetry sound.
He knows better, or should, to challenge
the status quo. Dough that he thinks he
doesn't need is the other helix's strand
needed for us to stand, and I don't mean
under, but over, if you please. A more
affordable view I'd ride the cosmos by,
charioteer, of a sky far from heaven,
it's true. The hells our dreams constellate
are paid for, purgatorially, would that

slopes be furnished with gold, not ash.
Alan, you've Dantean designs I hear,
and the lines I've read of yours echo
the maestro in one respect—salvific.
And Pacific mines you've had at, may be
emptied of its ore soon. The wares
of yours you've fashioned from fairy dust
may soon be just that—dust. Feel free,
though, to leave your footprints on this
topsoil, for those to come after you,
sooner than the blink of an eye, if not before!
My subject's the world according to me,
while your subject's the world according
to we, a fine madness, that is, for the loss
from ecstasy of the central, all-seeing I.
You won't get sympathy, though, out of me,
for in me there's none to be had.
Fidelity is no man's land I can defend,
except it offends the reverends of the world,
yourself included! Ha-ha-ha-ha!
Lots of luck cleaning out the stables
of our estate, Herc! Just keep it real,
meanwhile, on this our karmic wheel."

ii

"Dear Bots, you aren't dear
to me, but hey, be of good cheer, I say,
which, apparently, you are. How's your
star working out for you lately? The bar
is mine, as you know, the Guinness pint
keeping the likes of me on track. Shell
game is what I play. Hell of a point

you make, of making your mark
on the world; credit to you, a maestro
no one hears, or very few. Fires I stoke
are called competition, worth my time,
if not my rhyme: to each his own,
or whatever, brings it home."

Expatriate American Translator

(his voice)

i

"Alan, Charlemagne and his dutiful daughters had desire
down pat. We who identify can also, with reservations,
relate, even at times with gusto, as we're doing today.
The tumbledown effect is a principle at work here,
have no fear. To stick by friends is what friends do.
And porridge is for bears to swear by, not steal by,
honey bears no exception. What bears closely examine,
of course, is what the mind delights in, in search of a
steady light, whether lantern, or lamp, or lighthouse—
the ground to stand on or seas to sail in—in either case,
for the body to ship out on is the gears we wheel
into motion. What ho! The future brings us possibilities,
to which we now may look forward in amity!

"…Whether the ticking time bomb
is a dud, or will cause an explosion
that will rock our world, depends
on numerous factors, of course.
We hold steady on our course
in going forward, now to slip from the
berth smoothly out into new waters…"

ii

"Don't say the name 'Alan'—
he's game for whatever's the same,

Japanese-style. It took me a while
but he's got an authentic smile,
one he doesn't play others for.
Hands down the nicest man
I've met here in years. Honest
to god he walks his walk
and talks no jive…"

iii

"Shy he is, wasting no words.
I stroll the byways of my beloved
'Kura and snapshots open the view
for everyone to see: this, this,
this, this, this and this will be
that soon enough, so I'm in no hurry
to mark the trail to the next life.
This one has me by the dog ears
and happy I'll be to settle here
and there, or to the Wander
Kitchen go for the matching
whoever I'll meet eye-to-eye
there. For this is their land,
bye the bye, and I'm just
glad to live here a spell."

iv (their voices) (*from* Meta Frenz)

"He sizzles and simmers,
solaced by a reach I
still can't pinpoint.
Call it peace meal of
the gods. Where it's
going to take him, is

going to be a trip, I sense.
He lives for the imaginary,
not the historical, that
much we can see."

"Honors community, too.
Airbrushes his torments, too.
Socialized he's not, with a
pirated persona of sorts."

"Pirated?"

"Yeah, he won't own up
to being who he is. He's
too busy being everybody
else, methinks. Still, a
charmer and a cad, a soft-
spoken lad, and a teach all
rolled up into one. A lot
of bang for one's buck!"

"Salutations to our Asian
friend. He rocks the boat
where he is, that's for sure."

"Constantinople cries for freedom.
I like that. All bets are on, that
he harbors an animus about
how this place is run."

v

"Alan wavers between rich
and poor, hungry and

sated, doomed and saved.
I like the bouncing ball
in or out of his court.
The trouble is, does he court
fame or infamy? Therein
lies the rub. In or out,
clout or doubt? He seems
unable to decide. What a ride
his psyche takes him on!
The wheels now here, now
there, now everywhere but
where does he get off?
I mean, is his day the night
he tunnels through to get
to the other end? What
does he find, flying blind
through the night? He hears
things others don't, that's
for certain. I wouldn't want
to be the one behind the curtain!"

Enoshima Bowling Clerk

(her voice)

"The tall man enters our precincts with
a wandering eye fixed straight ahead,
wondering who his gaze will meet
and how he'll greet what he calls
the unknown. I know he flies
by the seat of his pants, for I've seen
him come and go, the half-smile
on his face older each time he visits.
The glance I'll give him is all he'll
see of me from the periphery of
the scene he makes as *gaijin*-man
who, before he goes, nods happily
to the camera eye we both are."

Japanese College Students

i (her voice)

"Alan we love you and hate you
but today let's split the difference.
It's a sad trudge uphill we go, for
a view that's soon taken away
from you when another story's
added on for the nth time to the
edifice next door, that grows
with time. History, it's called. Or
Babel's tower of tongues we all
belong to, reaching for the stars."

ii (her voice)

"Slit throat, we all know, touches
on what *seppuku* means to us here.
That's you, sensei, or at least representative
of what you're doing in class for all to see.
Immortality, you say, motivated you? Where
will you be next if not on our shores?
We wonder about our wanderer in our midst
from America, a country fallen on hard times,
like our teacher. But you won't hear complaints
from us. We hear your stories, listening as
hard as we can. Some of them go over
our heads, while others pierce our hearts.
Controlling the context is a shared enterprise
with you, in our lives a novelty we never

tire of, though some of us resent your
freedom and the liberties you take
on our account. But hey, it's English
that's your mother-tongue in our fatherland,
a deal we have to make, and we know
you know how it feels to have to earn
your keep, or bread, or whatever, by our
rules and regulations. And to swear
allegiance is our ode to hope. I do
that in the spirit of friendship, you
and me. Together it's a pact, if not
fact, of years long and in the making,
word to word, eye to eye, a holding
maneuver for peace's sake, and love's.
Loneliness breathes here, a roomful of
questions greeting it, and we meet
the terms of today with a smile and
a story or two. Is that you, sensei, or
a symbol of you? The poet and his
symbols, or is it metaphors? I'm not
smart, like you are, but arrows are
my words when shot from my bow.
Wounded warrior I'm not, for all your
Achilles talk. Never heard of the guy.
So much for immortality. But the point
you're driving at, I take. It's mine
now. Now what? Power wasted is a
flower tasted on a tongue that has sung
more men into orbit on the cheap than
all the dreams in your poetic sleep."

iii (her voice)

"Smasher's no masher, his moxie's foxy
and shines upon us all, eye to eye, with
a grin to match. We in his solar orbit are
stellar and rounding and when darkness
spreads we can outshine him any day—that is
to say, can spread moonshine his way.
He ebbs and flows as we rub elbows
with this stranger a bit strange for our taste.
Yet with choices limited, we have no choice
other than to keep rusing the tall *gaijin*
whose nose looks not down but across
at us which I'll give him points for.
The racket he sees through must have
exacted its price, but he stays cheerful
and nice. Can we blame him for being shy
and sly at the same time? The cues we send,
if followed, are clues which, as everyone knows,
make the world spin, so what say we begin
by obeying the rules and playing the game to win!"

iv (her voice)

"My teacher will bed me bright and early
if I twirl my hair and flash a smile. He sees
my coated candy and would unwrap me
if I have anything to do with it. Gorgeous
in my flippant way, I bend his knee
to my beauty in a glance. How becoming we
can be, at the first chance, were the moment
ours. But it's not, of course. He takes
his leave knowing the fence he sits on

cannot be climbed up or down. Where he
is, he must stay—on the fence watching
opportunities sail on by. It's called revenge,
sweetly, of youth. And one would wonder
who's on board the (fellow)ship and where it is
it's destined to go. Meanwhile, we keep our faces
on, meeting our duties of the day. Sunlight strolls
in through the door but the silvery moon's
eerie light softens its glare. Our eyes, bewildered
and bewitched, try to adjust to the shadowy realm…"

v (her voice)

"Botsford has eyeballs
bigger than his teeth—
I wonder if it's a sheep
or a wolf we've got in class?
He stares hard for such a gentle
bard. I've paved the road we're on
with a hardness of my own, on
loan from the softness he's enamored
of—love, in my book, is either both or
it's neither. That's why we're
eyeing one another across a crowded
room. He's got to have eyes for
me, too. I'll see to it that he does.
He's clear about being dear, I'll say that."

vi (her voice)

"The love boat you steer us all by
rocks our world, cool running
is the engine of your flow.

So where do we go from here,
sensei, the wave descent sheer
fun terror for us crossing the next
line and the line after that,
your lead we'll follow to
wherever our story will go,
one door opening onto another,
allure of unfolding worlds on view
we relate to you by."

vii (her voice)

"You're the best teacher our uni has seen.
You allow us to rehearse scenes we're
bound to be in after we leave these halls
and classrooms for good. And we all know
how bad it is out there, too, make no mistake.
Telltale signs of the way things are we've
got covered. It's the getting there, plus
all the details, that you let us in on.
And for that we're grateful. Dead-enders
all around us, which you're far from being.
It's when paths open that we learn best,
you've taught us, mostly by example,
never by preaching. It's a thrill from
beginning to end, and so remember you
we will. The niche of a writer who makes
for unknown destinations is one you fill—
and anyone can do that, too, you've shown us.
The hows and wherefores are for us to work out
ourselves, as best we can. Thanks for that, too.
Whoever said it would be easy? Our terrors
we've lived with, must be lived through,

we know: you've shown that, too. The real
faces we've seen in your green eyes are
all the proof we need. Seeding us a new
conception of ourselves in the furrows of
the imagination has enriched our lives
beyond measure. You're a treasure, the
greater for being well-hidden in who
you truly are: classy, and now sassy.
…You know who I am. That's all
I need you to know for now…And
that these arms that would wait for you
have charms of their own, which hereby
I own… O sensei I feel so alone."

viii (her voice)

"Alan you are a star after all,
would that we could go out to a bar
afterwards to see how far it could
take me, the light of your eyes…
But that won't happen. Still, so much
has happened to me because of you,
I wish I could tell you. To Italy
and London I went, and spent winter
break with my boyfriend, but that's not
all, so much more…It's come to an end
and I won't prolong our goodbyes.
Where I'll go next is what I'm dying
to know. It's been quite a show,
your zemi, and I'm not afraid
to say I'll miss you. Golden were
the moments when I look back.
Our uni I outgrew because of you,

but let it be said, never will I forget
how you afforded me, gently, your view."

ix (her—a different—voice)

"It's fake. The road he's on won't take
us out of the dark wood but instead into
a hooded truth whose unveiling will be
postponed time after time, those claims
all false that light up his eyes under any
but his own sky. Our goodbye was said
a long time ago and now it's certain.
Wash his face and chase the tears away
and what have you got? The part he plays
won't hold down any fort heavier than
the paper it's conjured from. He persuades,
however, by a presence I cannot deny.
Let him, then, take a stand among us
while the rest of us sit on the sidelines,
is the deal he makes, without stealing
a yen from us. I say bear him on our
shoulders for the joy he brings. He sings
up a storm in a field of daisies, the night
hatching the deeps shown in his greeny
eyes. He lies, it appears, to tell his truth,
and why not let him?"

x (her voice)

"He angles for a view
I'd freely give him.
If it weren't for you
Westerners, we'd be grim-
 faced, though we're young.

"He wears the mantle of savior but can't
save himself from what we all have
to live with, the dishonor of failure
hanging over our heads. Still, the wave
he rides in on every class has an allure
I won't deny, rippling like a muscled
body we wish he had, the soul he has
more than making up for the loss.

"He flares up with a light that shines
down on us all, and for that we love him
and follow wherever he leads, his energy
that of equal partners on this journey
we call poetry, American style, a force
to be reckoned with in our land of the rising sun.
Still, how little we can show of our feelings
which his presence calls forth, how small
our acts of gratitude for what he gives us,
himself mostly, with his sense of fun and fair play.

"Over and done with."

"No, just getting started."

American Editor

(his voice)

"He'll be roasted in hell before
we toast him, ha-ha-ha!
Toast boasts of an accomplishment
we won't recognize, and though
he'll go to the mats, or ghats, to
enflame our ash, silk-smooth and white,
it's to no avail. What's doomed
to fail, it's true, may have a tale
to tell, but it won't be heard by us,
that's for sure, at least not anytime soon.
Our course of comforts we'll not abandon—
not for a tombstone's worth of fame.
Nobody likes *his* leavings, kindred-struck
and inimitable though they be. We sold
him down the river no ferry can cross,
no spotlight's blaze can revive. Dead
to us are his abiding words. No 'big plan'
can break the stalemate of centuries.
There is no turning back, only we are
here, back to front, bottom to top
as what we can be, not renewed
but magnified by the glass through which
we look, and that indeed looks through
us—the blessed lamb and accursed wolf
retelling our story all of a piece, together
with the lion who's lain down his terms
for a peace we'll never know, while alive

on earth, anyway. Yet his story outliving us all
by a handful of stars ground up as dust
fallen through the cracks of time. Or is it Time?
Yes, mockingly the clock tick tocks
us into being true, to our unholy selves at least.
There's no excuse for eternity having its say
at anybody's expense but its own.
All the same, what an expanse he gives
us, a space in which to call not 'home'
but Time to account, to hear tell its tale
hooked like a fish out of water, its tail
slapping and wriggling on the banks before
slipping miraculously back into the stream."

Bull and Matador

i

Ferdinand the Bull was a story I
cut my teeth on, reading-wise.
For years the flower-intoxicated
hero accompanied me in my
dreams, or seemed to, for when
I had a choice of costume one summer
in grade school—a contest, was it—I
had on hand, sent to me by my father
on his travels, a matador's glittering
'suit of lights,' which I proudly
wore and was photographed in,
smiling, two front teeth missing
as I ate a popsicle, the photo
appearing in *The Washington Post*
later that week…

The 'matador' grew up, schooled
on America's gore, a lover
of books and poetry, and when
I met my beloved from Japan I knew
somehow, in my bones, she
would be mine. Though it would
be years before it dawned on me:
that I'd married a Taurus. The Bull.

ii (*from* Meta Frenz)

"I don't see how he can ruin
that marriage. He lavishes upon her
love and more love."

"It's a crying shame he has no fame.
What he's got, though, is a good name,
and to go with it gumption and game."

"What he's got he doesn't lose sight of—
a defense against rot and all it makes light of."

"He holds up, a bulwark; he's no blot
on the landscape, but an energy coursing through it."

"For him, once looked at becomes twice-told,
a harbinger of things to come, now bold."

Expatriate American Writer

(his voice)

i –after a podcast interview

"I settled in Japan to settle my debts
to my wife, who is Japanese, and for my
multicultural family to aspire higher than
adventure allows, the one we're on
morning to night, that I would not exchange
for anything, well, almost anything in
the world. The news poetry brings is what stays,
which I've done, with no regrets, to sing
multilingually of orbits I dance in
and out of, timewise, to make space for
my name, which I've got high hopes for,
a star shining in the darkness that others
can see and admire, that's the game,
isn't it, of fame, and there's no shame
in admitting I long to belong, once
I've paid my dues. Them's the rules
you gotta play by, and that's how I roll.
Which brings me to the present moment,
and the face I wear to meet and greet it.

ii (*from* Meta Frenz)

"Oh it's you who are running a steady
and tight ship. You've opened up
places, it's true, we never knew.

And for that we owe you, big time.
Humble, too, you are, for a star
we bet will soon be on the rise.
Calibrated to all sizes and shapes,
from formal to informal, it's too
good to be true, yet it is, beyond belief!
Radical ideas like yours will stand
tradition on its head one day, and
we'll live to see it happen, too!
Sharing the burdens while time and
space carry their cross—it's unheard
of, and makes no logical sense, yet
climbs the tree of reason by other means
where the fruit from the branch, when
offered, is peeled before our very eyes
and—lo and behold—multiplies like
fishes and loaves, sweeter for being
at our fingertips all this time. When
this is all over we'll have watched
The Creation from the prow of the
New Ark itself made of genuine wildness
and authentic rawness and abiding realness,
without giving anyone the shaft in the process.
Go figure… What lies behind that mask
is one who knows not to ask for the acceptance
we're not yet ready to give, nor have the
understanding to maintain it even if we did."

iii (*from* Meta Frenz)

"Art and society without the rhetoric of irony,
 is the name of his game, where poetry
 harbors no shame in dwelling in

certain doubt. In this he's
a f-ckin' wiz! From the cultural
humus he culls what the future calls for,
the vistas we've been waiting and
working for. The mud slung his way
on the wall of infamy undid the
fame he earned, but his will to love
remains intact—real tact required
of those saints among us, it seems.
 What profit a career that stays
in arrears, he's got us all wondering.
To redefine how the very sun,
moon and stars shine on us all?
Trust in trysts that won't go
bust, is a leap most of us don't
know how to make. He takes sleep
as his compass and leads the way
forward, or backward, or sideways,
or up, or down—as the case may be.
What he seeks is in how he speaks,
and we judge him to be among the freaks—
for he lets us steal his show… Whoa!...
This boat, I see, is harder to row when
he or we are doing so alone, so, all one
he tasks us to be, by trial and error!"

Descent (*from* Meta Frenz)

"The descent in the underworld is a male
or patriarchal myth—the son in search
of a reunion with his dead father.

"These journeys to the underworld
are happening all the time. Poets
give credence to the cost, in human
terms, of the love story we're all in.

"Every human exchange, to a lesser
or greater degree, is fought for the same
reason: you're the reason I'm here, we say
in hell to a loved one, the dead making
the living we do worthwhile.

"…Behave yourself, 'cause it's open.
Keep going. Doesn't it feel good
being part of the conversation?
It's where you find your new depth!
Uncomfortable is what it is, when
you're out of it—your depth, that is.
We're all paying the boatman
to ferry us across to further shores..."

"He was in this god-awful place,
but got out of it just in time."

"Homer had a bead on it long ago,
for all our Odyssean travails.

It's how time collapses in on
the wayfaring poets. It's the poet's
or lover's path, come hell or
high water, as they say."

"He doesn't need a table to sit at
so much as music of the spheres to follow
on his journey to ever new terrain."

*

History puts past the present,
the parameters of which circumvent
the future called down as infant
story, told and retold in instant
tableaux rising for time's fulfilment,
spatially forwarded as contingent
meaning, spelled now 'form' and 'content.'

"Cleo"

(her voice)

i

"Harm's way is never far
away in what you do, so please
be careful. The battles you've fought
all these years astonish me. I had
no idea what you've been up
against. The walls in our minds
being symbolic of real walls
everywhere you go, and you're
so kind, in the end, in letting go
the fears and the tears you've
gotten to know oh so up close
as to not be believed. It's humbling,
to say the least, what your East has been
for you, like sacred yeast for the
bread of Life, if I may say so, no
hyperbole meant. Where all this
leads remains to be seen…
I won't fog the glass you're
peering through to save yourself
and, who knows, maybe many others
to come. Godspeed and good luck
with the book, a winner—for all the
losses you've endured—you already
are in my humble book."

ii

"He's a bold man and maneuverer,
this one, and I'll let him know I'm a believer
but there are different ways, as they say, to skin
a cat, and where you're going with this
will depend on your having the perception,
yes, of a rat—that's traitor in Dante's lingo—
so you'll know what you're up against. Isn't
that what Art is all about, letting us slip into
different skins to know what it feels like, our
being fully human, since no one self does
the trick? …Oh! I see now what the trickster
stands for! It's to wear all those masks
and skins to rattle our bones, and to
know the energies of the universe come to
life while coursing through us at the same
time! It's the wizard's battle you wage,
like Sinbad on one of his quests we saw
on film as children. What a blast it is
to see magic make fast and loose with
the past. It's okay, I've pulled this curtain
back as far as it can go, and have seen
the levers being pulled left right and center.
Smoke and mirrors aligned with moral
consequence is no easy task, though, since
one's vision risks getting clouded and
fogged by others who, as you know, say
one thing and mean another. I'll help you
stay clear if you'll lend me an ear. What
are muses for, right? Lefty you are, it's
good to remind me. What a pitch you've
got—and the strikeouts will add up
to the perfect game you've got in you.

By staying small and keeping it real, so much
more to do, the next news cycle be damned!
It's news that stays news you're after, just
keep doing what you're doing, and the freak
show that is the subconscious mind will give
way to an alternate reality people won't
have seen coming! It'll open paths to doors
wider than you can imagine. But easy does it.
Slow is best, and while you're at it, when
gathering ye rosebuds, let them blossom
as you rise, rise, rise out of hell's reach,
and those vampires or zombies—call them
what you will—will lose their hold on you
as you're set free to higher realms of being,
becoming the man you're meant to be.
Time, now, for the mind to make its way, Ulysses,
back into the world again…"

Wonder

i

What to do when I am dead
is not what I had in mind
to find on my list of things
to do today, but here we are.
The humming I hear must be
the whole universe I am vibrating
with, or so Einstein said, his
space-time comprising a flexible
fabric that could be stretched and
compressed, bent and warped.
And the barely detectable ripples,
or gravitational waves, echoing in
the background now connect me
to the origin of life 13.8 billion years
ago, and I can live with that, no matter
(excuse the pun) how much space-time
there is left to me, to the self parlaying
these words into these lines. Pulsars
scattered across the Milky Way emit
bursts of radio waves which I have been
picking up for years, those comings
and goings of voices made from dreams,
it might be more accurate to say, but
who knows? My whole body is humming
right now, and yours too, from the tip
of your toes to the top of your head,
in tune with everything that has ever

been as we hurtle through the cosmos.
Yes, I can live with wonder like that,
to the beat of the trees' gentle swaying,
this melding of songs that we're
all a part of, our alling of the stars.

ii (*from* Meta Frenz)

"He wouldn't play by the rules
for fear of joining the fools
who became the tools
by which History fulfills
itself, in endless syllables.
He knew one more angry dude
would not be good
for the soul. Now it was food
to be made
by cooking up the hood
in his head
or was it bed?
that concerned him
most, verbatim,
before time fled
and he spread
his wings out loud
in the Hour of Lead."

"Something in common with gods.
Round and round we go
telling each other stories
we're never free of,
whose power it is to lift
us into new stories."

"Everything belonged to the
soul poet, so nothing did.
He hit his stride
on the way out."

"Even words received in a dream
are not what they seem, mixed
together hybrid of voices they are."

"Lose the solace of soul
and all that's left is loss
and its burnishing by time."

"A template for a future poet
is what he's making.
He overcomes obstacles to show the way.
A true pioneering spirit in poet's garb.
His entirety of language being
belies what as poet
you need to become."

"A metaphor for how to bear
the weight of history?
No, it isn't. But poetry
is the secret science."

'There's some beautiful flowering' (*from Meta Frenz*)

(their voices)

"There's some beautiful flowering
behind it, unseen,
to remind us new meanings
have a place to grow."

"Who knew this flower
had staying power
and the corridors
of the sick would empty?
The fort he holds
in his peaceful imagination
·takes all comers
at face value,
regardless of their
market value.
Shall we succor his depths
to sound more and more
before Time sacks him
of memory
and levels him
with forgetting?"

"His tropes of cosmic indifference
don't cut it here on earth
where heaven's cloth is stitched
with care and concern
for our brothers and sisters."

"All the same, such view
as he reminds us we have
restores that sun to the sky
under which all peoples
of the earth labor and die,
Shoah of history notwithstanding".

"His true kin is Dame Kind
in whose arms flourishes his body and mind
energized by what he finds
in her life-and-death bind.
Do we who are consigned
by reason to history align
better, or are somehow more refined?"

'Night's going away' (*from* Meta Frenz)

(their voices)

"Night's going away
into what he parallels—
darkness personified."

"No, it's a lull
in daylight savings rhyme."

"A blessing of
the becalmed storm."

"I totally agree and accept
their critique of the way
things are. That doesn't mean
we can live out its consequences
in the real world."

"The weight of hate
he's been carrying
would squash a lesser flea."

"The hind leg of the body
of Love he's latched onto
has brought him here."

"Time, perchance, for a
new host?"

"Or for a new way of
seeing the past, since
it sure as hell isn't
going anywhere."

"Shazam can turn defeat into
triumph if he stays the course."

"Whatever comes next, his text
will reflect a minor miracle
hinting at a major revolution."

"But the Street he's taken it to
towers over him. It's pretty grim."

"Sunrise has sunset
in his sights—only
to be blown away by
night every time."

"Peace comes on the wheel
of evolution, he's telling us,
or it never comes at all."

"Why take the fall
to get that across?"

"That, it appears, is his cross
he bears, and won't put down."

"How does he put up with
everyone putting him down?"

"On principle, The Great
Wheel loves all."

"Danger lurks where he works."

Japanese Professors

(their voices)

"He's some priest of a democrat.
He's some yeast for the soul."

"They say he can move stones."

"They say he is always alone."

"They say he's not afraid."

"They say he's not trying to get laid."

"They say he's true to his word."

"They say his word gets seen through."

"They say he wants others to get heard."

"They say he flies like a bird."

"They say every second
he's thinking how to go forward."

"At his throat is the institute,
but everyone's got a voice.
He wants them to have a choice."

"They say he's kind, and quite a find."

"They say the clock's ticking for our kind.
The battle's still young and the night long.
With us he'll never belong."

"Kore kara daijoubu?"

"We're going forward if he is too."

"Desk copy the poet poppy."

"He's no trans-god but he's a lightning rod.
Keep him in our sights.
We'll control who has rights."

"Does the world deconstruct
like this—with a bang?"

"Not as long as he whimpers!"

"They know that 20-20's
coming to fight for 50-50."

"His radar's pointed at the sky from down
here at the Institute of Love and Danger."

"We live inside words. He lives inside worlds."

"God the Father is the heavenly light.
May the best man win this fight."

II

'The world seems far away from here'

The world seems far away from here
as I try keeping up with the news,
but in truth everything I hold dear
depends on my keeping up with my muse.

To wormhole your way through
the universe and out the other
side would be quite a feat of
Imagination. And to think—
we do it every night.

One night the moon, full and hallucinatory,
shone a beam through the parted window curtain
piercing my heart as I lay in the dark, and I knew, then,
my muse of a lifetime had not abandoned me.

If memory is inexhaustible,
interiority is eternity.

There is no knowing a person
without the flowing of that person
into you. Language makes that possible.

Embedded in the language is a whole
way of knowing intuition
the way it was meant to be
felt in some fashion
or other, other being the key.

Responsiveness places the ball in your court,
even if death conspires to take the net down.

Get your heart out
of your mouth, I tell
myself. But it stays
there, and it tastes
like hell.

From it all, the agonies
we call throes and
the ecstasies we call flows,
nobody is exempt.

Wide awake,
unblinded,
history protects him
in the Grim
Reaper's wake.

The future belongs to history.
The past belongs to history.
The present belongs to history.
History *owns* time.
Except when it doesn't.

When they went through my body,
I felt these poems into existence.

I live in loss
I relish the dross—
leave the gold
to the hoarders.

Lowering the bar
to a stable
allows us to see
the star
we are able.

You bristle, as well you should.
I cannot exert any claim over
your turf: it's yours to defend as
you see fit. I'm just brushing up
on my native language, keeping fluent
in the boundaries we each patrol.
Border-free is where we'd meet,
of course, where we'd ride
the next wave to shore…

The first reviews are in—
it's experiential mysticism.

'He said, she said, they said, we said' (*from Meta Frenz*)

(their voices)

He said, she said, they said, we said
that the story is not over, far from it,
the story had not even begun when
its engine took over and what fun
if there was any we'd have—fit
for kings and vagabonds, and one
who dishes the dirt on who said
what to whom then and there
would be the one to tell us
when it was finally clear to say
he said she said they said we said
this is our journey into the woods
from which my cosmic I
mystically rose…

*

"Antlers on his bony body.
Headstrong, too. He's
crowned by life but won't
crow about his strife. He
pedestals beauty but wears
her shoes, too. A sanguine
affair of heart-mind and
body-soul together, steadfast."

"What every writer hates
is seeing into their inspiration."

"New field's
found labor."

"He turns poetry into patrimonial
and matrimonial struggles, an agon
for our times."

"Epic journey to purge what's toxic,
aided by sapphic and priapic energies
for the body electric and its view
of the world both poetic and scientific
in dynamic flow and interpenetration,
eschewing the cultic Freudians and
Jungians et al, instead embracing psychic
struggles of a Romantic bent neither
mythic nor historic, but anomalistic to the core."

"The catastrophic turn of events opened you
to your life, you were off to the races…
Marvelous things… overheard, Buddha-like,
frantically writing it all down whether from
waking life or from dreams, it was all the same—
horizons of meaning long neglected, now availed of,
the ground shattered beneath your feet along fault lines found
both deep within yourself and in the culture at large…
By symbiosis, osmosis, and synthesis moving
ahead step by step day by day smile by smile."

"We must let him pursue what
he sees and hears his own way,

entrust him with outcomes
unforeseen. It's the one sure
way we have of moving forward..."

*

The New World road, they say,
is open,
where the Old World road
is mapped all the way home.
Me? I have slowed down the show
business of my life to know
its granular glow, such as it is,
and to sow the seeds of ancient
theory in the practice of Flow.

'Let's do this'

Let's do this, I thought.
What exactly was it was I going to do?
Years of dreaming had fed the story
I now had in my mind, delusional to be sure,
but a story all the same, driving me unstoppably
to make decisions and choices in order to see the story through.

Bring it on: isolation, marginalization, silent treatment, hammer
blows, sucker punches, blind sides, verbal assaults, spiritual
welts…

…Admittedly it may be too far out for Poetry
and too far in for Spirituality and Psychology.

I sort out my experience
by means of the poem,
each further loss
of innocence
a step closer to home.

What would I have done, becoming one
with the Cosmic Sigh, but turned fly
in the ointment of Time, and spaced out
watching 360 degrees the expanding
and contracting horizons of my life?

There is no 'the story of;'
there is only 'a story of.'

It's all now
or never, when-
ever now is.

Jostling for the public eye, for public favor—

if it comes across as
suspiciously wide open,
it's because I've woken up
in the dead center of night...

These ideas sweep across
history and through souls.

You've made the unconscious conscious.
No. More than that. You've turned the unconscious upside down.
How is that possible?
Exactly...

What supernatural? There is no such thing as supernatural.
It's all natural.

There's no Mecca
for makers, only pain
of learning day by
day, what the train
of nights reveals.

The imagination of the poet,
which you're inside of
without even knowing it.

※

"There's no other way to phrase it:
he moves forward in phases."

"He won't be Zen-ified—
He won't be guru-ized—
He won't be eroticized—
He's wise to our tricks."

"He's in a border-free Wonderland."

"Revolutionary business."

"Yes, very busy."

"Erotics of politics
comes for us all, dividing
and conquering along
the way. Nobody is immune."

"Alan, true to his name, remains harmonious
in the midst of strife, a pillar of peace
for the foundation of no edifice."

*

Fleeing from battle,
I sneered at myself:
Peace-lover's paradise
is no place for us.
Back into the fray
I took myself,
dying to fight
to the end…

Diabolical

"diabolical urge to, well, mess it all up." – Lucia Berlin

It's no joke. It came over me, the urge, and
I couldn't at that time give it a name, though I can
now, the itch I had to scratch, of messing
things up that came from blurring my dreams
and my waking life, of east and west, until I
concocted a story which was simmering
below what I had long been sitting on top of,
that when words came, a volcanic eruption
followed, though I didn't know it then, a style
of poetic argument that dreams were made of,
that I secretly loved, a love that dared not
speak its name, a love of the urge to dream
in the face of brutal, brutalizing reality, a
diabolical urge to, well, mess it all up.

It was a way of thinking unlike any other
as I embarked upon a path of dream, and
was lost to reason but came to my senses
where memory of what had gone before
me opened like a door, and I was swept daily
into night's end, into dawn's new light.
Those sojourns deepening did undo me as
sleep undoes the dreamer, until, dispirited,
disheartened, depressed I fell past myself
to harrow the vale of Otherness steep, steep
in that darkness no soul survives intact,
so broken into otherness was I that I forgot

where others finished and where I began,
true to stars overhead that had led me there
in bloodlines I borrowed from books
veiny with poet's lore of stories read
under lamplight and cover of night, myself
nonetheless succumbing to the siren's song
beautiful for being half-heard under the waves
of desire, for pulling me to and fro in tides
that sought the outer shore close to the seasons
returning me. In. Stop-motion. To. The. Wheel. Of. Time.

"Not writing to prop up consensus views
of reality but rather to 'sabotage' those views
and replace them with an alternative vision,
perhaps radical but always sensible,
of what reality can be—inclusive and
empowering of otherness, even the most
marginal among us—that is simple, free,
exploratory, non-ideological, and cosmic."

Japanese College Students

i (his voice)

"Answer my question and you will see
how this mystery turned history
is planned spontaneously.
How else show you what conceals,
how else flow you what reveals
in less time than you can say "Love me
as I do you"? But the rhyme stretched
taut and thin won't work in being attached
as student is to teacher, for all cheeky
come-ons that meet with the inevitable,
awkwardly inescapable "Come off it."
We regroup and crew the next hardship
to shore unsighted, by candle unlighted
in a darkness of our own making.
For what spreads wide as argument is
a tide of words we cannot control
but that comes and goes, comes
and goes, as soul."

ii (her voice)

"He's as hot for us as we are for him.
He homes in on a frequency apart
from other profs, with heart and soul
on the line. He sits with his third eye
trained on us all, and worried not
where our looking takes us, even where
desire comes into play. What a dare

his class is, moment to moment, heart
to heart, the sad ones and the glad
ones, intermingling, interacting,
a course of small talk growing bigger
with each day, had we but ears to hear."

iii (her voice)

"Alan's Heimlich maneuver on the world
comes up short, but we love him for trying.
He says in so many words, Be passionate
all your life, the trail the heart blazes will
light up your darkest night. It's his way,
and could we obey, the world would be
an enchanted place despite our woes.
We grow tall just being around him, our Teach."

Japanese Nurse

(her voice) annual college health check-up

"You don't know me but I know you.
You're everything they said you would be, and more!
You can walk through my door anytime,
handsome man. I got my eye on you,
not just my paws. Lie down. Lift your shirt.
This won't take long… There. All done.
Now stand up. Time to measure your waist.
These arms have done a lot of wrapping,
and this job's easier with you to wrap!
I hear you nap and get inspired.
How about a quick turn with me, my chin
next to yours, my eyes locked on yours?
We're a pair, not a bad match,
if mating's your game. I'm married,
unfortunately, and so are you, I hear.
Still, a tumble for the two of us as we amble
out the door together, I'll lead the way
to where you go to next. Perhaps some other day.
It's as much in me as it is in you. We gotta draw
up a plan to meet, and I don't mean greet.
I'd have gotten to you closer sooner, but…
The right music, the right weather,
the right everything is all we need."

Japanese College Students

i (his voice)

"Now we're going round and round
it doesn't have to stop but
what are the next steps? What
new paces are you putting us through
and will we acquire a better view
by following you, are the questions
uppermost in our minds, Sensei.
What character are you developing
and will it be useful beyond these
walls and out there on the mean streets?
The lamb and the lion, Teach, each lying
with, or to, the other? I'd like to know.
Where does this go? The long
walk home whose coordinates you suggest
are plotted by everyone you meet
along the way. The day-by-day stuff
we sweat, requires a regular breeze.
We've seen crosswinds take you out
of the picture, so be there and be true
to us and we'll be there for you, too."

ii (her voice)

"Mr. Botsford, Moeri, not Moe, is my name.
I like looking at you as much as you like
looking at me. It's a good place to start, but
let's go slow. Where are these ringed people

they say gather round you? What ring?
The only ring I know is the one I'm waiting
for, by way of a bell—it lets me know
I don't need to wait any longer. Or
the tone of my phone they call a 'cell,'
not like this classroom we're all rounded up
together in. What say you to our own ring?
Just you and me. The one we'll form
not with our eye, nor without surprise, as
we go forward. But not now. Till next chime!"

Lost Near Shinjuku Station

—upon asking a woman for directions (her voice)

"This foreigner will be shown how
things work here. Haul him to the
koban for help and we'll see what
he does then. My trust goes as far
as my nose, and right now it's
twitching, rabbit-like, at his long
nose he's staring down to get a
better look at me. I quiver at his
attention but who the hell is he?
A total stranger! Maybe he's a wolf.
I'm taking no chances so the police
box is a sure thing…

"…Well, I'm impressed.
He didn't even blink. Told him it's
on my way, so I took him with me
as far as the station. Then said farewells.
Something tells me he's not your
typical *gaijin*. Still, better safe,
as they say, than sorry. Sayonara!"

Japanese College Student

(her voice)

"We had another day and the day was good.
A rainstorm blew in with thunder
and rain, and you brought us kindness
of drinks and ice cream, and we thank
you for that. You also have the patience of
a saint and the eyes of a sinner, both
which we love. We're not above joy with
you, and we're glad to let you know it.
If we keep it fun the work gets done,
and we all feel better, and the allness
is what the fun is about, don't you know?
We love teaching you as much as you
love teaching us. It's a shame you're
no longer young 'cause we'd love to make it
plainer what any sane girl feels in
your presence. We'll catch your eye
now and again and you'll catch our drift.
But it's lame compared to the real thing.
But it's not your fault, we know the terms.
The surprise today was getting the four frosh
girls to pant and giggle down the hall
and into the classroom! What a shocker
it was! What a whoosh of joy you swept
in on your broom of boyhood, though fully
a man you are as we can attest. Manly
you are, and womanly are we. It's a cockfight
or catfight to get your attention, for we

all want it so bad. You're not our Dad,
so be glad you're not. We wish we could be
bad… but…oh just the thought is rad!

"Alan we'll say your name over and over
and talk about you when you're not around.
We love you and that won't change. Thanks!
Pompous you're not, you'll get praise from us
for keeping it real, like a deal cut
on a stormy afternoon in late June 2011."

American Poet (*from* Meta Frenz)

(her voice)

i

"He nurtures our palship which I'm
not onc to abandon at this stage
of the journey, far and away the
most satisfying one out there,
and I mean out there! But he
inheres every step of his way,
a feat he'll one day rue or be
rewarded for, I'm not sure…
For he'll blow the Man down
if it kills him, and he has been,
many times, killed, which perhaps
eventually he'll say in a more public,
read: less private, way.

"Dr. Shoelace, is it scary out there?
Hip Hop Central he waxes on and
on about. If feeling better is what
it's about…
          Okay, there are a lot
more shots being fired! People,
so many people running in the streets…

"To say beauty is impermenance
is to be redundant, but he's bringing it,
right now as I speak…

"See if the seer's in the sewer again…

"He won't make a beeline for the mountaintop
but advances and retreats accordingly, his way
of climbing is in the so-called fourth dimension,
or so he claims. He may yet be venerable
in his old age, but his beauty is his cage."

ii

"Alan has hunches he honors,
so I'll honor him, in the humble
voice he has. How he holds on
to his honesty in hours of lies
is the timelapse into hominess
I'll give him credit for. We who
are wired for more, more, more,
won't settle for any less, lest
he harbors a newer port I can't
pull into. Pretty his boat is, I'll
admit, that travels the distance
with the likes of me. His Penelope
he honors, not altogether oddly and
has juice to spare, so I'll hop
aboard and see where he goes."

iii

"Alan lies close to the bank
of the river he's part of,
dipping his face in the water
like Narcissus, only he sees
the images of us—all of us—

being reflected there, and
sings us into being before
we part ways. He's a true
particle-wave poet. A quantum
mind among us who seeks
to find, not bind, otherness
on its way to becoming more
other—a salve for the wickedness
the self congeals around, self that
feeds off, not feeds, otherness—that
stain we all live with and die by,
in terms he makes plain. What he
won't do is call us out, for compassion's
sake, so we walk all over the grass
that grows, yes, in his wake.

"Tulip's his favorite flower? because
it's got power to sing! We know
the distilled hate brings, as his fate,
a tower of Babel he's building on the fly
for us to spy on. He whispers, and we
sigh at the work he undertakes, while
we fake friends rake in the spiritual
bucks, and with it, the shirt off his back,
a Prince by any other name. Yet name-
less is not without fame, just a game
to keep it fresh. I'll water his name
when spirit moves me and rhyme
installs us. For now, nature calls us
gently down the stream…"

Fujisawa PC Repairman

"Who's the *gaijin* pulling up his car
in my driveway? It's dark and I
can't see him well. Let him come
closer, and my pet Lab can get a whiff
of him. Stop him in his tracks, she
will… He won't bow, or only a little.
The one he's with, his wife? is one
I'll talk to, who speaks my language.
I do my job and tell customers what
they need to hear, to fix computers.
I know the arcana of that inside-out
world, which never fails to surprise.
My posters of Japan's Self-Defense
Forces prominently displayed on
my walls, the model tanks and cars
on the shelves, and computers old
and new stacked up on the counter
all lend a disheveled air to my shop
out in the boondocks where I work
and live, beside a field under a new
moon…Time for them to be leaving.
Though the *gaijin* be friendly, saying
so in my lingo would be bad form,
so I'll just see them off with a bow.
You're more than welcome to call
any time if you need to consult me…"
And the darkness enveloped them all.

Expatriate American Editor

(his voice)

i late

"Time-lapse photography doesn't do justice
to the mind of yours at work, slow-motion
for the details to emerge, fast-motion for
the bigger picture to be seen, and I for one
am impressed by its motion to love things
as they are, in a generous, life-giving arc
from dawn to dusk, minus the clichés, sir.
We bow to such an imagination, and will
welcome its activity on our pages in future.

"Audible silence the cacophonist creates
to win readers to his side that he calls
'other,' one we can now see better
by his stoic efforts and poetic insights,
the gun-lovers among us notwithstanding.
He has to have developed a thick hide
for all the troubles he's endured, though
you won't hear him complain, which makes
him taller in my eyes, a prize specimen of
a 'mamaist'—native through and through—
in our midst, soul-tested tried and true."

ii early

"Bursting on the scene
won't get you seen: Ta-ta!

We ween authors on, not off,
the kiss-ass bottle around here,
battle away all you want.
Hocus pocus loses focus? Soak
us in your wavy dreams and
see where it'll get you. Ha-ha-ha!
Drowning you out takes a nose-blow.
No place for modesty where
you are and will stay. Niceties
my ice, a cold burn for
the meltdown you espouse.
By the way, who owns your house?
You'll get nothing but grouse
from me, and no further in
the Welfare City. This wrist raises
a fist whenever you're around. Best
get used to it, and cease and desist on our turf,
here where gays gauge the winds of history,
Arabs wage war against the Jewish story,
Blacks rage against the victors and spoils of history,
poets and sages think they can change history,
while girls, above all, have no place in history.
For we males defend Power with our sacred honor
and collage our wits to engage in making history…
That's the lowdown, as low as you'll get it—get it?
Beat it! You'll never beat us to the punch, Judy!"

iii

"About the author—
funny, integral, halcyon,
deeply embedded in otherness,
in the whys and wherefores

of human exchange.
A load he's carried for years
and survived
to tell his story,
a fabulous attack on
the corruptions of our age.
He pulls no punches
but goes right for the juggler
of the self as we know it.

"The sea will come in words,
a sea of otherness
that boggles the mind
and structures one's imagination
to new places.

"The poet as pretzel,
twisting and turning
every which way."

'Air reading Japan and dreamcatching America' (*from* Meta Frenz)

(their voices)

"A true indivi-dual, with a lineage divided between
a decadent Italian aristocracy, gold digging Irish,
and cosmopolitan Hapsburg-German Jewry."

"A supernova telepath poet who, in hypnagogic states,
realizes we are in the process of dreaming each other awake."

"His heroic, oceanic, psychedelic radiosphere is
a subliminal pastoral of epic dimensions
on multiple channels of choral surround sound.

"He lives in a cosmic diorama as a pacific man
in a transparent world—air reading Japan
and dreamcatching America via infernal dialogues."

"Perhaps flowers in the soil make the world grow."

"Harm's way he stays out of now shows what
he's been through with a vengeance, a poet's
fate if ever there was one."

"He alleges that there are forces at work
in the world and in the psyche—each
mirroring the other—that are natural,
cyclical, and empirical which may be

observed by the subject with both clinical
detachment and love, simultaneously."

"What you're overhearing
is an under-war."

"The miracle of science
revealed
in the mirror
of art."

"His music of poetic thought leaves in the dust
the voice of logical reasoning. Is this why 'churlish'
Plato banished poets from his republic?"

American Professor

(his voice)

"There is an arrow pointed
at a target. He lets it fly
blindfolded and each time
it hits the target, nay, the bullseye.
He is Odysseus in rags, dressed
as a beggar come home to claim
his throne, were anyone watching
and waiting. We're not, and
we won't be bamboozled into
believing his cock and bull story
and the lies he sings. Still, give
him credit for the ruse of his muse
that tall tales are born of.
What I wouldn't give
to live the life of this Reilly!

"The sun shines brightly
where he steps lightly,
and I don't mean poetic feet.
This guy brings the heat
we can only dream of.
Conflagrations galore
he goes to war for,
is willing to whore for,
drills down to his core for—
it's a showtime I'd die for
were I of a mind to live for

the ideals he goes to bat for.
Crumbs that come his way are for
the birds, he says, which he's thankful for.
Who is this guy?

"These lines instill in the reader
a fearlessness not to be believed—
the world's heartlessness taken to task
and its rot dismissed with a restlessness
matched only by his selflessness.

"I'd sooner die and go to heaven
than harrow the hells this guy has done,
all for a future won,
he thinks, under our shining sun,
while mooning us in fun,
he says, done with utmost devotion.

"Sheer inevitability he climbs
up or down, in the guise of rhymes.
Wake up! Wake up! he shouts to the times,
words which everyone nickels and dimes.
Who can blame us for our petty crimes?"

'A Hemingway of his life' (*from* Meta Frenz)

(their voices)

i

"A Hemmingway of his life,
each chapter is suffused with
wisdom and folly joined
together at the root."

"He knows it's the only way
he can grow into the role
he makes for himself—
outsized and irrepressible.
The kids love him for it—
he breathes life into their dreams."

"Horrors he's been through
makes wholeness he aspires to
an all or nothing game.
He lets himself be played
to stand up to the co-opters."

"This is my daily grind—
exhumed as nightly finds.
Be still, my heart, or
palpitate artfully."

"God almighty. But I don't
know what to do with it.

It does nobody any good if
I don't know what to do with it."

"He writes in his sleep,
his soul to keep.
What he wakes up from
he calls the home he
can never go back to again."

"The conceit is, You can see it,
the transparency, through and through."

"The chain reaction of one thing
inside of another thing, inside
of another thing, caused by
a freedom too great to bear,
and too far-fetched to believe."

"He drove his story into the ground.
but it wasn't lost to begin with
so how can it be found?"

"Yup, you are
ungovernable.
We're not sore.
It's your lore....
from your bottommost depths,
it soars!"

"Who has time for this?
Tropes are my bliss
to take me sky high.
I do so without reservation.
Try my war cry

out for size. We
diss the featherbrains
of this world, while wearing
the headdress for the rain
dance to bring it on.
So get ready! I'll not
throw confetti your way
any time soon.
My people unpeople
at high noon
would-be steeples like you!"

"Into the sea of origins we go."

"One brief shining piece of evidence
against a backdrop of raw data."

"Years and years of golden tears,
how many only he knows for sure."

"Other men would melt down
to the core of disillusion and loneliness,
but he rode the molten swirling lava
of love and dubbed it 'the open road'."

"A strong consciousness
conscious of itself—
that's the way of the ancient Greeks."

"You're not searching for
the unity of the universe,
you've found it."

"Discoveries of the
soul's plenitude."

American Poet & Critic

(his voice)

i

"A figure, man or woman, reaching
into their bag to pull out a pistol
is the vision that rises up as I read
his poems, the pistol a stand-in
for his obvious power, the gender
ambiguity pointing to a deeper
ambivalence at the heart of his
language as he parses his emotional
landscapes with tropes meant
to test his fortitude, if not his talent
for blending time past and time present
as tokens of his survival into a future
his words make, one sentence at a time,
grasped not in a temporal unity but
spatially reconsidering all he held dear,
all he held in fear, and all he would revere,
now glossed in the margins of his world."

ii

"An argument against human meaninglessness
so profound as to be a revelation where
basic decencies prevail and grace rules.

"He lifts the lid off poetry
and finds depths of spirituality
living there, actualized as soul.

"Has, if nothing else, a message
of hope, but there will be many
who can't be bothered to care.

"Rabbit cuts loose in the care of poetry,
tortoise bags the prize in the name of mystery,
while eagle-eye watches over it all.

"Identity he decries is in the service
of bigger fish he fries.

"The poetic temperament personified and embodied—
no mean feat, with cajónes to spare.

"He marries discovery to exploration
at their roots, called the unknown.

"The very definition of friends
is they help you get out of trouble.

"What shall I say?
Say whatever your heart
compels you to say.

"The doctor said his old wise man
routine won't wake anybody up.
But the candles he's lit will stay lit.

"Animosities galore. He won't
whore around to avoid them.

"Ditto politics.

"He left these shores to open
new doors to the other side.

"The individual self has limits
he imposes on it. That said,
where he goes with it, only he knows.

"What will my father say? 'Stay safe.'"

iii

"A definite breach of trust
that civilization is built on,
and yet with unmistakable reach
into hidden places where is rewritten
his core of being.
Out of hiding he comes
bearing such gifts as not
to be believed. Colloquial speech
he masters belies the disasters
he's faced—and how!
He's got us covered as well,
his ordeals he won't directly tell
but only indirectly, letting others
speak for themselves, unheard
of in poetry's precincts
in more ways than one. He's won
our hearts in the bargain.
And for all he's been through
he stays small, on call to his muse.
He corrals their happiness into lines
before setting it free onto the plains
of sight and sound revision

for a world wider than it was,
now attuned to imagination.
To their art of loving he remains
true, known as You."

Japanese College Student

(her voice)

"Whose look can spruce up a book
better than mine, who pours over pages
like a waterfall, nymph that I am?
Bright is the trail left by my waves
on the shore of each paragraph
you'd skim, for hopes and desires gleaned
from darker depths of your lifelong sentence,
worded from the tip of my blood-red tongue
into a story I'd make deliciously our own.

"Tallied by the road I'm on, by signs
I heed or turn my back on, my worth
will not be subject to your whims.
What I can see will see me through
the illusion you'd insist I be for you.
Plying my trade, I'd bring on fate
by what I've made, and will make, at
the altar of your beauties and charms.
But I'll not throw myself away or in harms
way as the object of your curiosity or
diversion. Next time, genius,
is one that you'll be ready for.

"What pulls apart what's poles apart
is already the visible outshining

the invisible. That's my job,
to tease, like you do, meanings out
of our collective hat worn in an act
staged for the benefit of those who'd watch
with saliva drooling how deeply engaged
one can be with one's peers, how the psyche
can gladden its garden east or west
that grows in a soul's healthy soil…"

"…I told you, I'm eighteen! They
make you want to write a masterpiece,
but hey, who are we kidding?
I've lifetimes to go before I get
a real piece of the action. Meanwhile,
I've books to read and reports to write.
I'm in the dark needing a light.
Who's going to be my spark tonight?"

'Imagination is nothing' (*from* Meta Frenz)

(their voices…)

Imagination is nothing
but butterfly-winged
air seen through,
turning and turning
as kaleidoscope of hope,
which in its wake
might leave a stain-
glassed window more real
for its light-sparked view
of the darkness ahead.

*

"For the would-be psychic pathfinder
no way forward is safe. The going
gets tricky when things from below
bubble up to the surface, and things
from above sift underneath, and presto,
the topsy-turvy world insists on new meanings.
The trouble intensifies, moreover,
when the status quo pushes back.
The psychic turmoil that ensues can
easily drown all but the most stalwart
of mariners, and even they can
expect to pay a heavy price."

"We mustn't blame him. He's a poet
among us. What can we do?"

"Have him try on somebody else's shoes!"

"Yes, but—ahhh—with him quickly pass the hours."

"Are you trying to make another
description of me? How dare you
even try! Words lock us in
place, where we lose face. Spare
us your writings, leave us
in silences more loyal to our
truths than your promiscuous words!
Faithless poet! If you are no longer
American, you are still not Japanese,
sorry to say. Hey, we don't make
the rules. Fools who try to break
them pay a price heavier than
you can ever imagine, were you
to try. We live, suffer, and die
here where our parents, grand-
parents and great-grandparents
lived, suffered, and died. This is
our native land that no native-
speaker will ever understand.

"I'm the boss of that, from here
to here, and from ear to ear!
No loss will deprive me of my
right to ownership of who
I am, not you or you or you!
I am the cumulative effect of
the journey I've been on since
birth here on earth, and sky
or no sky I am each step taken

in the dance of my life, that no
one may appropriate or assimilate
for sale or for borrowing or even
for bartering. I am not in circulation
for an exchange that you control.
No, not at all. The circle I'm in
is of nature and for nature, where
man, I hereby declare, has no
longer dominion, nature free
of man being my true nature,
my inner nature if you will. For
in this dream-charted territory
man is but a guest, a visitor
perhaps, but no less a guest,
however reborn from the bone
blood and nerves that keep him whole."

III

'It wasn't the first time'

It wasn't the first time
he stood before an outdoor altar
wondering if it was two claps
of the hands, then a bow,
or the other way around.
He tried both on different occasions,
letting the moment guide him
so as not to offend the locals
sure to be watching.
But pray he did, to the gods
sure, he thought, to be listening,
a faith, yes, he had ritually put
in words.

Say of god
that it is
sky of gold
Say of god
factors the X
in every equation
Say of god
hums the song
dying into light
Say of god
imagines all
that is real.

Now the turning becomes you
and takes you to an endpoint
you didn't see coming, where
vision declares a magic of moments
regathered from a light far away
but getting closer every day,
a parcel of land you walk on
and tend to, where footsteps anchor
the spirit on its quest for the crucial
and the receptive, like a radio bandwidth
tuned to after an earthquake
to hear when and where the tsunami
will land, if it lands, as you make
your way to higher ground
following instructions heard,
were you listening, on the frequency
at which survival is pitched, but
faith needed to climb the summit,
whose generous depth you won't
be forsaking any time soon,
gotten to by a swoon instigated by,
say, a poem on its way down
to the particulars of time and place
remembered in a vertigo of language
dizzingly grown from a pencil
whose point leads you in the direction
of where you've been going all along,
a mind at odds with itself in a body
you believe in, if not worship at,
given everything you know now,
and everything you don't.

Do not go to god
shimmering in the waves
Do not go to god
riding the crest
of the fallen
sky, or waste
your breath at the door
that is closed
Do not go to god
on upright feet
basking in the sunlight
whose heat
you endure until reborn
in the consuming fire
Do not go to god
dancing in attire
at nightfall
soon shucked like corn
Do not go to god
Oh do not go to god
unless hopelessly
out of the mire
arising, like a flower
on the back of an empty hour
which on all sides
announces, You have nowhere
else to hide.

The ecstatic nation,
the interior the land
of otherness, the exterior
the land of strangeness,

bounded on all sides
by a sea of selves.

Make no mistake, not one god
but many dot the landscape
of one's imagination, yet I wonder
how many selves have I had stripped
away, how many lives have I left.
How many truths have shattered
my soul, how many lies have
shuttered it. No one knows better
than you, I tell myself, whose view
is less than panoramic but offers
clues that, in this instance, you
don't miss, how it all adds up sooner
or later, to a conclusion reached
not monumentally but humbly,
a silence momentarily breached.

*

"He is a seeker of truths
he can't see but hears, or overhears
by nights he invites, tenderly,
day after day, music painted on air
canvassed cosmically, where voices
rewire the soundness he's made of
to retire, here and now, into roundness
he keeps close, not closed off from,
like the garden he steps gingerly in,
back of all his housed and harrowed years."

'He's looking to be more solid' (*from* Meta Frenz)

(their voices)

"He's looking to be more solid."

"There's no shakier ground than the unconscious."

"His poetry's inspiration, poems coming thick and fast,
wherefrom a mystery to him no more…"

"If sex were the basis for all human behavior,
and I'm not at all convinced it is, but if it were,
then this recent, channeled poetry does it justice."

"*Diabolique* environment."

"Sexual energy gets transmitted into dream life."

"So Freud was right?"

"Yes. But remember, he used Greek myths as guideposts.
Here we have a whole different ballgame, where everything's
blown wide open."

"How so?"

"These energies translate in many different and new ways.
Channeling voices from the 'other side' is one thing; but
overhearing people's unconscious thoughts 'live' as they

speak is a whole different ballgame. And dangerous, too…
Your own death. It's quite possible."

ii

"Can-doers and won't-doers mingle
here, call us "friends" if you like.
What we're watching for is more
of what we do, less of what you do.
That's the sum of this non zero-sum game
you play. For us, it's all or nothing
and you got nothing, like it or not.
The game's ours, the rules won't bend,
not even to mend what needs mending.
Too much is at stake, for one. Too few
can wake, for another. Sleep is preferred
to the cacophonous waking you'd call for.
We sow our oats and get off—oohhh yeahhh!—
on a status quo too long in power
to let go now, honey bee, flower
all you will. Our will rules by
wordless agreement only we adepts make.
You're not one of us—bottom line. But, hey
Sailor, I'll take you for mine if
you row my boat ashore. Ha-ha-ha-ha-ha!"

iv

"Life-affirming schlock rounded
by a cosmic spin. He genuflects
at the altar of celebrity without
pining to become one himself.

"He feels his way line by line,
which says something about the
man's intuition, a prize he seems
to have fought for, that few
recognize. Credit him for fearlessness
in the face of neglect and incomprehension.
Clean as a whistle, he offers us
a bag of tricks free of charge, gallantly.
…OMG! He's wilder than a wetback
on a wall! He swears by anonymity, too!
A pearl-diver maxed out? …Yes, into
the next life, it seems. He's a bridge-
builder to other worlds. He clarifies
mysteries without giving them away.
He's a sorcerer at the core of Being,
collaborating with the gods. Fortune
abounds in the realm of imagination,
he shows, making us less afraid of
the unknown."

"He goes on and on extemporizing
in the key of Emerson, time
wormholed once more."

"He shuns his own open heart
that beats wildly for a hearing,
informed and reformed by art
altogether monstrous and searing."

"We're saved by the balls
we have to have, but even then
the falls we have to endure will

pin us up against psychic walls
beyond our imagining. It's nowhere
where mortals can live long, that
I know. Catastrophic fears faced,
non-stop. It won't let you settle
or rest in your identity but keeps
you harrowingly in the stream
of identities, subject to inhuman
laws of Imagination. Psychic
endurance is what this is about,
not magic. It's exploratory at
the borders of reason and faith,
never before in this form or
of this boldness. It's one scary
motherf-cking ride he's on,
and don't we know it now."

"It's not sex but sexuality
his work explores. He
makes the distinction
necessary and illuminating.
Eros has the upper hand,
but no moral high ground
claimed. It's what
makes it all so human."

"Like a diamond, every
personality has facets."

"His crystallizes around
the desire to know, and
the knowledge of desire."

"If you want to know what happened to him,
read what people say. But what
people say, is not what happened.
Where does that leave us, you wonder?
Yes, it leaves us wondering!"

American Editor

(her voice)

"He's not who he says he is.
Being what he is, though, by his
lights the House of Art is built
from the floor of Hell up,
a charge of libidinal energies
coursing through it…

"Dangerous to a degree unheard of.
He posits a lifeline to the unconscious
that is thousands of years old. Nobody
dares follow him. There is no
imagination equal to it equipped
to survive the pressures and tumult
he has had to endure. Language of
this order is preposterously original
and trailblazing. He asks only that
his poems be admitted as poetry.
He doesn't rue the price he's had to pay."

*

Human, that's all I ever wanted to be,
said the poet. Little did he know
how difficult it would prove to be
as he went out of his way to show
what he was made of, exponentially
raising the stakes with each blow

he received, to his notion of humanly
possible, which caused him to grow
into what he was meant to be, he
realized, far, far from the status quo.

No one knows what I know
to be true, unless they open the door
and, taking my hand, go with the flow
deep inside, to where there is no shore
to stay on for long but that'll show
the wave on wave particular
words that carry us far
into the beauty we are
for each other, to grow
into new selves nice and slow,
above us like a star.

American Poet

(his voice)

i

"I see you're still doing things out of
the norm, your new mamaist
poetry opened my eyes to what
kind of life you've been living
in Japan, such a traditional, poly-
theistic culture, and the way you
relate to it is astounding, it informs
a mythic consciousness infused
in all you do in daily life. Quite
remarkable your way of presenting,
say, the life of Eros from the inside out.
You've adapted to Japanese folkways
with a Western skepticism, and arguably
maintain a connection to and strike
the right balance with presenting
the bigger picture. The book captures
the blessing of a cross-cultural existence
lived deeply, psychologically rich
in insight, spiritually adventurous
in courting 'come what may.'

"The trail of years won't be taken
by many—it looks dark and dangerous,
and can you blame them? We poets
suss out the forest growth for the

unexpected animal to be our spirit guide.
With you, though, it's taken to
a different level. Readers want to try
and take advantage of your gifts, not
have to work for it, which is what
you make them do. No easy path
you offer—making the unknown
your destination of choice, turning
away all but the most intrepid readers."

ii

"The heaven he haunts us with
on earth is not entered by dint
of good works per se, but upon
realization of one's task, to be
undertaken fully, devoutly even,
until one's dying day."

Japanese Psychiatrist

(his voice)

i

"Alan-san closes the door on mystery
and wants in on our history. What to
say to him except the battle lines
were drawn ages ago, and no one
wins a place there who hasn't been
born a Japanese. So soldier on all
you will, closure is a windfall of
the poet in us all, hemmed in on
every side by the face of the god we
call 'Japan,' a false flag waved front
to back wherever you dare to go."

ii

"Alan-san softens and plays it
at his 'own pace,' a man not worn
down or hardened by life, gentle
and, beside the river he steps in,
finding mirror images to coast
along, the mode of the poet
with a zone to be in and embody.
The lines on his face betray
such softness as pure pleasure knows.
The calm shows, and sits well for
the turbulence he's had to navigate

of late. He's making repairs
and puttin' on no airs, just following
his 'my pace' to take him where
he needs to go, calm, cool, collected
making sure he gets there, the face
of a man come into his own, feeling
at home with who he is and what he does."

'The violence of a word' (*from* Meta Frenz)

The violence of a word
sutured to a page
—without it, where's the future
of peace in our age?
Tear the veil from what's heard
and you'll see inside the cage
the true nature
of my singing bird.

In the end, who we are
is what we say when
what we say touches
the core of our star.

Daylight carves out its niche
in the darkness, ultimate destination
of hours and minutes circling
within us, and about us, sculpted
from sky and morphing clouds.

    (their voices)

"Policing this beat is he whose
feet don't touch the ground, in
a feat of imagination riding
psychic energy from one end
of the beat to the next, feeling
the heat like a Shaolin monk
trained by the energy of the stars.

It's time we got the show on
the road, is what his subtext says,
obeying the context's rules while
reading the spirit's clues. Whose?
Depends on where he is, and
for how long…"

"This bruiser has come far
without a car, cruising in a
vehicle of enlightenment.
His gratitude without attitude is
refreshing. He lights a
candle in the dark.
And I, for one, can
see my way clearer for
his having been here."

"Simple—like music."

"He promises to enter into
a new relationship to his
history's health."

"Inalienable rights he claims
for the visionary in society,
doing the vision thing in
political landscapes as well as personal ones.
He favors the fight."

"We're not different in kind,
only in degree—the poet
and the politician.

History and desire, mortal
enemies only in captive eyes."

"Returning to help out
exorcises those demons."

"People were not interested
in other people."

"It's not news,
but newsworthy play."

"Chews you up and spits
you out, history does,
given half a chance."

"This does not sound like
a human orchestra.
It sounds more like waves
now rolling,
now crashing ashore."

"Holy smoke
of divine fire!
How does he live like that?"

"Serial monk won't
womanize his way home
but with safety net
in place, balances
on the high wire between
east and west,

the conscious and
the unconscious."

"C'mon, homeless.
Where's your
Homer face?
Constipated are you
on the Milky Way?"

"Size increases
dark matters
when we steal
the prize!"

"That's so you know.
Who the hell says
go slow? Not
on our turf."

"For the fighter,
this is the perfect
time to live in."

"That's enough, he says, of the power-usurping ego
bent on destruction of the sources of creation.
Time to start over before it's too late.
I'll give him credit for ambition in the name
of soul, knowing what it's cost him, and
cost us not to hear him. The irony is that he's
completely helpless in the face of the world
as it is, yet he presses on. I want to educate
my son, he's clearly saying, for the teach he is
has global reach. He'll settle for one or

the other, teacher or student, as if his life
depends on it. And shame on us, it does,
we not knowing his name in the flow of fame.
The paradigm he hitches his wagon to is one
we're all related to."

American Publisher

(his voice)

"Holy is his head, and wide his art.
The body of his work will spread
its message to the heart.
I'm not grumbling. What
you see, he says, is what
you get—and it ain't
some tall tale, nor
a whale of a story.
A school of minnows in
the wake of the
shark is more like it.
He knows the world's a dark
shadow that no arc, narrative
or otherwise, can outsail.

"His 'here' thrills our 'there'
with music of a love up and coming
through the fog of war, misery
and daily devestation.

"The club has rules he aches to break,
sunny-side up. This dumpty
has humptied enough. Take
him out with one shot.

"Bambi bamboozled us all once,
but not a snowball's chance

in hell will he again.
Snake-eyes has gone
underground but he's far
from done.
The fruitcake he'd have us
believe he is, is no rummy
but an incisive mind full of
wit and humility.
I've never seen such a combo.
Snake-eyes has a focus
I'd beware of, though,
it's intense.

"He doesn't need to grab
the ring each time he
comes round. i.e. on this go-
round he's content to show
his hand and say, I pass.
He lays low but is clever
with the uptake. I shudder
when he gets too near:
that slider won't hide his rattle."

    (their voices)

"Who does he think he is, Bam-Bam?"

"He mocks us with blocks
stacked one atop the Other—
it's building time, he declares,
and nobody's willing to knock
them all down unless he
does it first. And strangely,

he has and will again start
from scratch, round and round he goes.
How does he do it, I wonder?"

"He interprets the poet he's not
as the poet he will be.
He misses the mystery of life
so he sets traps that'll be sprung
each spring.
The jell he solidifies into
from the river of his wayside cell
comes from the torrent he swims
against, deep down within.
It's how he reaches out, celibate
that he is, like a monk
repeating his prayers at different
intervals of the day and night.
He had a twenty-year stretch on the prowl;
now he just howls. It's a hoot!
But the heart he shows us
has its own flow—
wild, passionate, savvy
and irreverent all at once."

"It's a boon."

"It's quite a bouquet."

"It's an array of Ways.
But Jesus knows his Allah
better than he does.
And if he buddies with
the Buddha, it's the budding
that happens when he's around."

"Holy Mary! The limb he goes
out on is likely to break,
and him along with it, if
he's not careful. The cache
he's earned may get him burned
if acrobatics is what he's after.
That Tropist had better hope
for more and settle for less,
at least for now.
The Trackers will be on his
trail; we'll know if he bails."

"He climbs the summit to eye
the view of us all *together*—
a scary breath he takes
of rarified air up there,
I'd be lonelier than Han Solo.
(Hey, are you listening?)"

"But his Princess Leah is Gaia,
don't you see?"

"If that's so, that's some flow.
Cosmic and masturbatory, his ardor?"

"More like whatever sphere he's near
he absorbs, then projects onto his inner screen.
He sides with whatever's opposite him,
less hide-and-seek and more see-saw.
He motions out of love's emotions, though.
A neat trick, for the renewing work it does.
The Self's mitosis births myriad
selves that'll never add

up again, except in imagination—
that's his reality."

"What holds it all together?"

"What holds it all together is
the cosmic grapevine he eavesdrops on
and he hears us all by.
Angelic, telepathic, either way
it's epic, in its way."

"I'll pray he stays.
For his tricks that stick,
like ardent sex without bodies
that he recalls being like Love's Body."

"It's a leap
the Tropist takes
in his sleep.
Nothing more to it.
And it's nothing less
than human and stupendous—
the difference we all make
splits reality down the middle
at the seam of dream
and imagination."

"But what's real?"

"The turning Wheel—
he knows the real
deal when he feels
One."

"Heinous crime
not to publish him,
but it'll stir up
a hornet's nest for sure."

"He weeds the Garden
of Eden, I kid you not."

"He won't count
the cost to him and his life
nor rue the day he answered
his muse, yet is shameless
in nakedness."

"The places he goes to
are summits and cellars
of the soul
he gives his all to."

"Deeply traumatizing to boot."

"How does he survive it?

"Strange hungers
of the human kind."

"And a kindness
that grows with each poem."

American Editor

(his voice)

"Dream friends forever.

"Sweeping away all that
came in the past…

"We've been trying to
have this conversation.

"OMG he's having it
layered and profound.

"Fine texture of sand
in an hourglass.

"Does he grow people
in his imagination like
this, or overhear them?

"How much of this is real
and how much imagined?

"He cannot erase the borders
without serious consequences.
The ramifications are staggering.

"God help me.

"God help him.

"Its Odyssean curiosity
can be led astray.
He knows that
and makes provisions,
its foresight matched
with insight of the ages.

"I heart this guy's
poems but not his path.
How can I? It's monstrous
in the extreme.

"Out of the cave
bellow Cyclopses too
numerous to say.
He tempts the fate
that provokes or
inspires him.

"Bogus muse it's not.
Lotus fuse that's
lit to illuminate
the underbelly of
our lives.

"A huge stride forward."

Japanese Dentist

(his voice)

i

"Alan-san holds the candle
that lights his darkness, but how
much can he see before the
flame is extinguished? Crosswinds
come down hard on the heart
opening and closing on a breeze.
I know I wouldn't want to walk
in his shoes, not for all the money
in the world. As it is, he smiles and
sheds nary a tear, while I gouge
the poor sod. He's no friend of
mine and I'll let him know, business
is business. Still, the thrill of living
in a foreign land seems not to have
worn off for him. He's not shy
about its strangeness infatuating
him. Twenty-five years and the romance
going strong! Plus a song he has
to show for it all, too, sonic
improprieties aside. What a ride
he's on, say what I will. He greets
me and 'greats' me with his toothy
grin. I grow fond of him in spite
of myself. Where he sets foot on
my turf, I'll remind him, is thanks

to my hospitality. And to make it
a hat-trick I'll add that my women
know his game and think he's lame.
So long, no-name!"

ii

"Alan-san has a son that shines
and who wouldn't be proud of him?
As a father, you should be. It's what
we're made to be—pride ascending
into a heavenly fire all can see.
We men know the place women
want us to have, and we abide,
but never on their own terms.
It's our terms we dictate, word
by word, and it's a catch-all
of a discourse I run in my shop.
Here I piece together a wholeness
by my training and standards, and
it's a long day's journey before night
ever calls the shots. It's not that
I don't appreciate what darkness
sheds, but the light I believe in
is what I'm wedded to, a union
I won't forego under any circumstances.
The will—my own—is the bill my fate
collects, and I pay dear for the show
to go on, horsepower be damned. Trotters,
canterers and gallopers there may be,
I'd best them all by my willpower,
whose hour is time redeemed in my eye.
So, see as you like, what you like, east

or west, what I know would set
your teeth on edge, chattering ad infinitum
towards a natural condemnation of
all things natural… Now you see by my lights!
The fall you take turns ball I throw
at your expense, which is no mistake, given
the terms we live by. Near perfection
is dear to such as me, glory in flaws all you will…"

Expatriate British Editor

(his voice)

"Alan's cajones are conjoined to the air
he breathes—a breathtaking duality
he's won from battles I can't begin
to fathom. How, earth-wise, does he
survive the costs borne in the name of
what? Poetry? Love is too grand a word
for me but he takes a shot at the cosmic
sun in which Spirit basks, so who am
I to ask? Still and all, a helluva way
to get to heaven, if you ask me. These
isles have made mincemeat out of
worthier men, but none more loving.
I wonder if he's got an ace up his sleeve?
No harm in keeping the door he walks
through open to a future I didn't
see coming, nor one I'll foreclose on."

Japanese College Student

(her voice)

"Alan in here and Alan out there
he upholds the law and tears down the wall.
It's unheard of, his world worded anew
through a dance behind the scenes.
We'd refer to what he refers to
if we could, but what's a metaphor for
if not traversing the gap in between?
So, he engages the cages inside and out,
barring none, despite the bitter cuts
and prolonged ruts. Shame won't adhere
to his name in the game he plays,
casting no blame where others issue
false claims against him. He gets got
less and less, for the rules he masters.
So be true to Alan and he won't rue
the day he let you in on a passing view
we see of a heart palpitating in growth
humbly, and, humbly, sharing its wealth.
What beauty gives, is truth received.
This I can say in Japanese, affectionately,
his warmth felt through his loyal student,
were I to be heard in the public ear,
dearer for sounding a human tear."

American Editor

(her voice)

"Alan hides in a world of his
making, and who am I to dispute
the boundaries. Heaven and hell
I've heard he's traveled, yet
joy radiates from his face. Who
are we, in the end, anyway? Certainly
not our past, any more than our
future. The present we give way
to, for sanity's sake, but his radical
notion of present defies even sanity.
So where does that leave him?
Leaves of grass he'd bed down in,
and my money's on him reawakening
in what we call future time. Until
then we'll give him a platform
to speak his truth. What a truth it is
time will tell, and space jell."

'The poet is a loser' (*from* Meta Frenz)

"The poet is a loser, says the poet
whose losses have added up to being
a poet who doesn't want to lose
more ground to the poetry of seeing
his way in or out of the close
quarters his poetry puts him in—
the spirit he travels through to get
to where opens both time and space
as hymns, sung to the body arising,
for love too true to be good
or bad, but celebrates its own wedding
to the here and now, its faithful muse.

"Yes, to outsmart the trickster, the father
feigns a family wooing its blood ties
and flies not in the face of reality
but to a place farther
away than even he realizes
by an agency all his own?, one he prizes
for making distinctions uphold
the gap between them, which he chose
to keep us on *his* toes."

Carpenters At Work Next Door

"We housebuilders have nothing but contempt
for the *gaijin* among us, who builds
nothing but a prefab monstrosity on
top of a hill, one we can see clearly as
being built on his family's shoulders,
owners, like us, of this land, while he
reruns what's original to us, a Japan
sans the man with or without a plan.
For our land will stay ours, so… politely
we'll invite him and his ilk to leave,
if not our land then our sight. It's our right.
Show us the temple of your night
and what have you got to show for it?
We know where the sun shines, and
for how long it will shine—not on
our dime will shadows crawl and creep.
Ours is a daylight labor of love, with
history to tell it straight: we are
what you are not—a Japanese, pure
and simple. Go back to where you came
from, is all the sentiment from us you'll get."

"Cleo"

"There's our poet, but now's not a good
time…because he might be overstressed
which, being a Westerner in the East,
tends to happen to sensitive types. Alan,
a poet of the Wheel of Fortune type,
what goes around, comes around
and all that—is hard-pressed to keep his ears
from picking up everyone's subliminal
urges and impulses. I know I couldn't stand it,
but what he's doing is surreal—dreamlife
infused by everyday interactions, so you
see what's happening from all sides, but
you're not sure what's true and what's
made up, everyone's got their own view.
It's a hoot, I'll say that! Instincts herded
into poems by voices overheard, while Alan
stands to one side innocently observing it all.
It's unheard of, but so's our poet, Japan
where he lives and works being as remote
as the moon, and just as unreal. Did we even
go to the moon, is the question Alan, in his
poems, answers for all of us, reoriented to
where language takes us, those distances
traveled in words that defy space-time
continuum as well as gravity. He hears what
his antennae picks up and it's a lifetime of
scandals, his school is, which rhymes with
reality dreamily, in alternating currents—now
dreaming at night, now dreaming in daytime…

It won't sour you on East-West relations. To
the contrary, one revels in the music of the dance
we humans do around and for each other, mis-
understandings et al. Alan desires an Ark to take
him the distance narratively, but I say he's lucky
to have survived the flood and been washed up on
Japan's welcoming shores. Let critics and other
readers open doors to his house of the rising sun!"

Japanese Professors

(their voices)

"Tasted our spleen but is not
wasted by it, he is stronger
by far than he looks.
The façade he wears is
oddly triumphant, if withdrawn,
creating a silence we all
can hear, whose richness is
beyond compare. We'll only
proceed on his dare, and
stay tirelessly aware."

"He is an intense presence
among us, it would do us
well to remain cautious
and return in season to
suffer his moods. Let
the knife blade of his vision
cut through the walls we've
built to keep him out. It
won't matter one way or another
if we're gotten to, now that
he knows the rules we play by.
Win or lose, we own the
playing field he stands on,
and this he knows, he knows."

"We see him as a spectacle
and nothing more, certain
are we of the insignificant
part he plays in the overall
show. Whatever we say or
do he now knows is an act,
and that's a fact. We won't
bother to deny we're all in
on the pathetic sham of the old
swallowing the new, powerless
we are to stop it. He will see
the limits of desire and make
no further attempts to take
us higher. We know our place
and now, thankfully, so does he."

"Culture wars in the U.S. have
nothing on us warriors here
in Japan, having fought
our own for a millennia."

"Sift through the ashes all he will
for a glimpse of the future, the
future he sees is one we seize
before he is a part of it. Teach
stands his ground, though,
that's clear. And lights us,
if we're lucky, with his good cheer.
But here the past has reach far
exceeding any future you care
to imagine. And to it, everyone
but him will bow."

Hayama Café

i —waitress

"Indebted to the stars,
the firmament wastes away
but for the beholder's eye.
Yet two eyes don't make a scene
unless imagining what it's for,
late or early, by the light within.
Still, without the body as door,
no open or shut case either,
housing judgement there.
We seem to be, or be to seem:
a feminine wile in a masculine
fantasy, our betrothal your
acceptance, a marriage
of minds to make or, yes,
unmake as the case may be."

ii —waiter

"He rattles his bones,
the *gaijin* ghost does,
in precincts not his own,
a haunting we abjure,
were it not for solemnities
observed, for propriety's sake,
reckoned for a piece of the pie
served, and consumed, here,
Japan by any other name,

a calling he heard once,
no doubt hears still, host
of abundance in the abyss
whose voice he answers as his own."

iii —waitress

"The strange man in the corner holding court
over a book, careful with that one, his eyes
peer at you as if the world depended on it.
And it does, were he half-believed. We gals
know what to do with *gaijin* customers, even
or especially if they speak a gibberish they
call Japanese. Each glance is our parting gift
to the moment overflowing to the next, and
the next after that, a chance to test our skills
of evading predators on our turf. But hey,
that's half the fun of being one—prey I mean,
in the souped up world they occupy for
free, if we'd let them. And we do! Go figure…
The view of Fuji-san he takes in with a relish
befitting he on foreign shores, is, it's true,
unbeatable, straight across the waters and past a
cloud cover that rings the stage near the summit
with a shining aura only a god exudes…
What sin we would get up in were our stage
set differently, our pose—mere subterfuge
for the lies we'd tell, of a boy-meets-girl kind—
our pose we must maintain in the face of
their supposed lust, one we've heard so much
about concerning *gaijin* on our Shonan coast.
Better safe than sorry, we understand. Still,
the electricity in his glance betrays no innocence

that our experience couldn't top. For now, we
take turns meeting his gaze and keeping our distance.
Besides, as we make our dutiful rounds he keeps
his head mostly buried in his book. Some show
he'd have us on, when nobody's even watching!
…Gets up and walks out, he does, before any of us
can get noticed. Umph! …We'll hold the door
open for the next *gaijin* customer who comes
our way, for the 'welcome' our eyes will say."

Nepalese Writer

(his voice)

"I clear the lens of my mind
and write what I see. Poetry
cannot be faked. What I would
give for a poem that moves my
soul and reflects the stars in
the heavens. I aspire to *be*,
first and foremost; *then* I write.
Clarity and precision seem to me
worthy goals when putting pen
to paper. It's true we're not long
for this world, so make the most
of your chances. Ambidextrous I
am, both east and west, though
dreaming-wise, east is a beast.
West puts to the test all my flunky
notions until water can be drawn
from my inner well that's not
muddy but clear and refreshing.
It's what I aim for, at least. Senses
lead the way to whatever edge
I arrive at. Crossing over is what
courage is for. I hope to have it
each time, or woe betide my soul.
For east or west, boundaryless is best."

Japanese Professor

(his voice)

i

"Botsford has amends on his mind.
He catches the wind and rewinds
the film he's been watching, to where
the givens of our time and our race
are not taken for granted. Would
that he take steps like these every day.
I fear his night, however, will dawn,
leaving us out of his equation, the film
once again fast forwarded out of
the prison cell of our precincts into
some peace-meal of wholeness we'd
partake of together, separation be damned.
So that's his game… A rewiring
of the brain whose circuitry goes
round and round, here or there just
the same no matter who does the mattering.
A trifle imaginative for my taste.
At least he's no opium addict, but will
follow my edicts issued in his language.
He'll be taunted, his telltale sighs aside.
We'll be haunted, though, by his eyes—
the look they give timed to a river's flow
that empties onto our sea only
of tea and sympathy, and no more."

ii

"Coffee cups mingle our breaths
as we rest here together. Sip
and eat as we talk the time
away, the buzz in our ears a
metaphor for bees being beesy
and combed in wax. Cold is the
sound of my voice, as history's
muted and breathless bone
testing the waters of the present
with each of the twenty-four
hours as ship's crew. Who knew
Time would take us to these shores
to reach what we long ago set out
for—peace and friendship, a golden
age for cages lived in, space
it's called, across or through which
we move in word and in deed,
the dead shadowing us each step
of the way. Did you think it would
be otherwise? Proximities ghoulish
or kind, now haunting, now taunting,
lasting lifetimes. Enjoy the view,
with the new context you're cooking up
but a text buried raw in the sands
of time, left behind like a beach
at sundown, to be drawn back
like the tide at dawn… What galls
you are the gulls squawking for
a piece of the action they may never
get, let alone deserve, those noisy
pigeons of the sea, however dovish

they are in constitution or costume.
The Hinamaru, meanwhile, raised
gloriously above the islands of Otherness,
announces our identity in waves."

Japanese Professors

i (his voice)

"Botsford-sensei, the wireless companion
over airwaves east and west you are
and have heard tell about, which isn't
politic to mention, but you, I hope, will be
our go-to-guy when we're in a pinch,
which is now. The sliced off ear van Gogh
gave to Gauguin isn't half as juicy as the earful
I hear you gave to our peers at our uni, but
I dare say they deserved it, and you my respect,
if truth be known, for what I know about you,
and what I don't, which, to be sure, is
armloads. The heads we nod at one another
will have to do what our words cannot—
cross the cultural divide. My thanks to you
will be forthcoming, now and into the future,
that I can guarantee. The rest, as you know,
is up to the powers that be, albeit as power-
grabbers-to-be. So, beware. In solidarity."

ii (his voice)

"Botsford-sensei won't say so but
the poet in him chafes at the bit
teaching Japan's youth at our uni.
Where would he go at his age, I bet
he's thinking, and can you blame him?
A job's a job, we've all got to have one

to put bread on the table and roof over
our heads, he'd be the first to admit.
The slander he's endured has served to
douse the fires he once had burning for
the classroom. Still, a class act he is,
strong and able, doing his duty today."

iii (his voice)

"Botsford-sensei, sly poet, recoils
from our proceedings, sits quietly
observing and listening, wonders
from his wandering imagination how
to pinpoint meaning on a map
to make the journey and back
where the day leads, his fellow
travelers as foreign to him as
he is to us, he being American
by birth, now decades in his adopted
land, we making room for him
in our midst, twilight years awaiting us all."

iv (his voice)

"From hear on in
I have no history
apart from a question
put to my purgatory—
'Will you raise our
children by the hour
and fit the schedule
as no pearl nor jewel
but what for us

is the outspread lotus
on the surface of waters
for our sons and daughters?'
You have shown loyalty,
it is clear. That's enough
for now. We'll seek camaraderie
when the going gets rough.
The rest is history
joined to testimony
of the outbound mind
whose expression, genuine
 in every way, is now signed."

Japanese Support Staff

i (her voice)

"Botsford-sensei relishes the chance to chat
and who am I to deny him that?
He segues from self to other
in the wink of an eye, but to mother
him in transit is not my job.
He gets too entangled for my money
and has an eye, I hear, for honey
—eye-candy, they call it. They don't mob
one as old as he, though, not so funny
were you counting the years on our shores.
He's opened way too many doors
to hell and back that've done him in.
Still, a sad song I don't hear him humming.
That said, it makes me sad to hear
he lost all he had, or almost all, from
the fall he took on our watch.
What makes him, nonetheless, a catch
is his willingness to learn, not snatch
power from the unsuspecting
the way most *gaijin* try to do.
For that he earns my respect."

ii (her voice)

"Haggle we won't. This is our job.
Prices in our market rise and fall.
We'll sell, either way. No buying

on this turf. He's handsome, but
as his hair recedes, so will I. One
of us will return, however. What
cow-like virtues he displays I'll
portray in his mirror for him. It's
the least I can do. Though in a
different time and place a bull
taken by the horns would be, ahem,
in order. Sigh… Border-cross on
somebody else's archipelago. I've
got Kei Nishikori to root for, don't
forget, who everyone's gunning
for. His are real horns—world-class
ones—that I'd gladly dub bull. He
is who he can be, not wish-on-a-star
far but here in your ear near.
Surely that ringing sound in your ear
can't drown that out? I'll lie, by the way,
till I'm blue in the face, the only clue
I'll give you on this case. Sherlock
had a home in my sleeve, ace.

"P.S. How we relate is not to identify,
which is what makes you Yanks fly.
When you say hello, we say goodbye.
Tell us more, Teach, if you dare try."

American Poet

(her voice)

"It's a mindscrew.

"Sleepy man I once knew.

"Traffics in the Dead
to live up a storm
in what goes unsaid
among the living.
I don't know how
he'll get read.

"Among the 'Have gun, will travel' set
he's pulled off the upset
of the ages, pages and pages
of the stuff he won't get enough of,
it looks like. What it does to
the psyche is anyone's guess!
To say yes is to no more
and fear less. Jesus!
A sweet man, no less.

"Approval's stamp he wants
but won't get, everything's
up for grabs in the 'not yet.'

"Funny how the mind takes over
for the big newshound
who plays dead but won't roll over.

"More and more he teaches
the apple of know-how
is within our reach.

"Trippy how he stays sane beside it all,
waxing and waning.

"A culture in the round
is what he's found,
a culture of sound
that's deep in the mind.

"He rips the culture to pieces
and puts it back together again
to show how wonder never ceases.

"It's no mistake.
He asks for nothing,
we give him nothing
as he drives a stake
through the culture of our time
in the space of a rhyme.

"'Size matters'
lies in tatters
as the universe twitters
in his ears.

"In lust he trusts
to get an earful of the West.
How the price he's paid must
gall him, trust or no trust.

"He killed himself
and lives to tell the tale.
He wills himself
not to fail.

"Will you love me
I want to know,
with me as the mystery
you'll want to grow?

"It's the Sixties,
will you look at that!

"A man of many minds,
he's in love with
whatever he finds.

"All's well that ends well,
say what we will—
he's found a place to be."

IV

'Let praises be sung' (*from* Meta Frenz)

(their voices)

"Let praises be sung of mothers
and daughters. Male power not
thwarted but a residual structure
the poet occupies for the duration
of the poem, for his own purposes
and ends, which is in part to loosen
the very structure in which he dwells.
Astonishing feat of imagination,
the transition from niche to destination
captured in language poetic to the core."

"His idiom is done nicely—right
between the eyes of the culture.
It opens up your saints
buried deep inside you."

"We got magical wires we
dangle from all the time
keeping us suspended in
language, he tells us, for
places unknown, were we
to dare to go there, with no
guarantees."

"He must miss the U.S. mighty fiercely,
yet won't say so outright.
It's pretty cool how he takes on
Japan the way he does—telling it
slant, in more ways than one."

Foreigner

On native ground, born outcast
(if only to the center, that holy ghost
I'd have guessed at, were it host),
the sound I sound like most
is mostly foreign to me now,
thirty years on, on which I bet
my life, a gambling man I'm not.
Losers dream on, says the poet.
I've been dreaming on, lost
to America, Japanly. But
note the circle where the past
comes, if not full, finally
after the eyes straighten past
the horizon, duplicately—
what the first will do, to last.
In this no matter its cost
the die seems cast,
of the foot in a step discretely
as space and time once kissed.

Expatriate American Friend

(his voice) (i.m.)

i

"'M.' here. And here I'll remain!
No crossing the Styx for me, not now
at least! Though Charon's nose appears
at the misty shore where I am…
The East has a river all its own, which
dogpaddlers like me wade into at our own
risk, one you've obviously not heeded!
Drowning noises poets make may get heard
in time, or not—that's the risk you took
with your Whitman book, I now see,
so eloquently the passionate plea for freedom
it was, and is, and will be (if I may say so,
jealously…). You won't hear me gurgling
this out loud, but only in your dreamstreams
where lurking are dangers of many kinds—
one foot ashore, one foot in our fellowship
notwithstanding. These waters running deep
are for silently running, don't you know?
Unwise for them to be heard, save for over-
heard, which is all I'll do for your dreamy
view (read: your uncanny 'you'). Please a
shadow I won't, I'm too old for the agon,
especially when other agonies attend me
daily. Where does whining end and defiance
begin? If only we could separate the locomotive

from the caboose—Twins pulling from opposite
ends of a train on the same track, sans motive!
But the dead, I know, come with the living
wherever we go, a withy coupling of spiritual dough
with the too-much-with-us-worldly show.
But if every current has an undercurrent, who
can tell which comes and which goes? And
what separates a creation myth from
a cremation myth, if not a spelling of 'I am'
from beginning to end?"

ii

"Alan I'd have you over for tea but eternity's
been knocking at my door. Better never, I say, than late."

'You can take it, or leave it' (*from* Meta Frenz)

(their voices)

"You can take it, or leave it."

"That in itself is a feat."

"What is?"

"Honing in on the aperture
he presents, of his view of the world."

"His is a world radical by
any measure."

"Heroism defines him but he
won't be defined by it.
He refuses now to play the role."

"Conscientious, soulful, and
untroubled he seems, and
the dreams he has are rich
in creative power and love."

"Japanese sunlight barely
blossoms forth, but he
does so abundantly.
I'd like to see more,
much more."

American Professor

(her voice)

"An explosive, dissident take
on contemporary culture east and west,
in a working space unlimited in its scope
as it ranges freely across generations and cultures,
agenda-less, yet for the sake of newfound health.
Each sightline he takes a bead on
he draws sustenance from.
He genuflects at the altar of time without end
that is poetry, a vehicle for opening space up
and populating it with the living and the dead,
equal partners in a dance we're each part of,
where the historical meets the cosmic under
or behind the words that the poet sounds,
his own self both fluid and compound.

"It establishes individual voice as a mutable idiom,
rather than insisting on style for its own sake.
It allows one to explore gender and identity beyond
the ordinary limits of the poetic voice. It raises
the possibility of ever newer terrain to be explored
by poets and writers in descents into the unconscious
that, as he shows, waxes and wanes in more than
forms we think and write by but as wheels of balance
at play through deeper truths that sound in his work—
how the death of the author gives birth to the reader,
who in turn writes her way to form again in an endless
cycle of culture at home in nature, and vice versa,

as radical a belief as must be read to be believed,
yet beyond faith—all this and more at stake.

"The aperture on closure widens
to encompass failure, to see
what lies behind and under
the plenipotentiary…
imaginal fountains
in whose waters
you bathe refreshed,
allowing life to draw you
into your love and learn from
the challenges. Death, too, has lessons to teach
—which is your fear of it that gives it its power.

"May the terms
of the argument
forever be alive.

"Strengthen your mind
with this find.

"You can be funny
without being trivial
You can be teacherly
without being pedantic
You can be scientific
without being arcane

"Love the space you're in,
and your time will come round
(in compatibility mode).

"The landscape love enlivens
is both inner and outer, and
closer than you think or see.

"The sky you look into
has a depth you can't see.
Pray time will heal
the gap between
you and the stars."

'On this boot train'

Before I get
there I'm not
even here, is
how not speaking
Japanese feels like
to the one
who speaks Japanese
in, yes, English.

In the space
of a time remembered
the face will change
and the heart rearrange…

On this boot train, I'm just
following the tracks, high-stepping to
the music of my dreams.

Steamy vegetable vigor?
All I know is, Allah is the champion
of the hajj. One push up,
and it will appear, the flower
of existence. It will always
flower into existence just as
things are, no more, no less.
Watch the flower of existence
anchor itself in being and becoming,

each moment a new petal.
The bed of roses one keeps
to one side, to better
protect the newest stems and
shoots appearing, the appearance
it's making eternal, until the next
new stalk of appearance takes
its place empowering the now
and new, hoisting up its flags
of readiness, waving with unabashed
joy and confidence in its Being.

Unable to hear myself think,
I've turned around and around
until the latest music of the spheres
was heard note by glorious note,
the harmonies and point-counter-
point awe-inspiring, keeping
me mindful of all that is here
where I live and work and play,
all this that is where I am going
to be the next round, the spinning
round in place so as to reach all
that I am, with hands upraised,
heart open, feet on the ground guiding
me with no authority but my own
to write my story true to,
and to lift newer stories into hearing,
a sentence at a time. Who are you
to be true to, after all, if not you who
are spinning now in new directions
the tales that will define and liberate
you, both at once, as a story you are

writing into existence? Hello oxygen
wherever you be—let me breathe free
to empty myself of days gone by,
and to welcome what's coming into
being with open arms, turning and
turning on its own mystery....Yes,
listening to all sides, filming what I see,
'The camera doesn't lie, but you
do' is what I read, and know is true.

Reading Class

i (her voice)

"Botsford-sensei writes himself into
our minds without lifting a finger.
How does he do that? His smile has
wattage, but imprinting on us is
his age, despite all his best efforts.
What do we gals want from a man,
after all, besides his looks? His spunk
and his fidelity, neither of which we
can expect from our teacher, or
only so far, that is. The rest is up for
grabs, as he shows us, a roller-coaster
of a ride, as we know from stories
we've heard. He settles down, though,
on turf as old as time, which we here
in Japan claim is mythic, the basis
of our emperor worship. Yes, we
stay loyal to a thousand-year lineage
because that's how time binds us
to it, and to one another—in a sequence
uninterrupted and in a space that echoes
us all. That's why we can have
a ball at his expense, his American
free-for-all the subject of our suspicion,
if not derision, since no such gall can
last long on our shores without ending
up in a perpetual shortfall. If I were
him, I'd be climbing the walls, which

he probably does despite his dawn's
early light. Anyhow, it's too late
to rearrange the way things are
that will last beyond the sunset
where, sadly he'll have to
walk off into, and into our dreams."

ii (her voice)

"Alan's hearing his angels again
but it's our hearts that are ringing
with the sound of their voices.
We know by now the tunes they sing,
a chorus we join at our own peril.
Still, without them we've nowhere to go,
and he knows that, too, or seems to.
We'll follow, then, wherever he leads.
It's the least we can do for the most
we're dying to be, so help us goddess."

Reading the Air

You read the air because you are one,
atom, that is, of many, circulating in
an atmosphere changing as you speak,
non-being being put into play just as
being plays down what it's becoming,
so you get a view of yourself together,
of a piece, appearing circumstantial,
peripheral, integral as the case, open
or shut, may be. Judging from the reaction,
though, silence on even molecular
level, washes away regret as you smile
to yourself, and let things go their way,
ten thousand of them were you counting.

*

To sustain the experience of what we call the Self,
I needed to learn the language of fissures, crises, breakdowns.
But spiritual practice does not a 'system' make.
Without an ego, where does one go except,
Odysseus-like, into the unknown?

*

"You'd do well to stay where you are."

"Handsome eyes have the big reveal:
a loved man."

"In training the I is, to all forms
of otherness. The result is not
mastery, however, but acceptance."

"Ancient values at work do not undermine
the modern so much as throw it into relief."

"Shaolin recovered opens a world
to the uninitiated, profound dimensions
of energy flows."

American Poet & Editor

(her voice)

"The Web itself is an endless
media apparatus, global in reach,
as Botsford mindmelds with others
to create his poems.
He stops at nothing
to capture those voices.
The result is a new
kind of lyric poem.
Or rather, it's not a lyric
at all but a synthesis of
many voices which he
conflates onto the plane
of the poem until a chorus is heard.

"I'm saying his approach has
startling ramifications for
poetry as we know it.
His voice is that of a
many-selved consciousness.
He's in the driver's seat
of the bus while saying,
Why don't you pull over
and come up?
It's the antithesis of Eliot. It's
no fairy tale, it's more like
a cultural upheaval—it's
an in-your-face, staggering
reversal of history."

"I slept with my lover and found
my way back to the kingdom,
is what he's saying in so many
words. The life of the spirit
embodied in his poems makes
the human experience rich and
full and whole, in ways not seen
in contemporary writing. This
journey will beggar the imagination
and enrich it beyond words.
He dialogues with other people
both living and dead, and the result
is as surprising as it is tantalizing.
Where would it lead us, to follow
where his song goes. He offers
the ride of a lifetime for a chance
to find out. We brought them back together
as partners, he tells us, of the
mind-body conundrum.

"The bile flung out at him.
The bile hit him between
the eyes and he didn't blink.
Dead meat most people would
have been.... I wouldn't know
how to present this book to our readers.
We'll determine the outsider's role
in due course."

Japanese Poet

(his voice)

Alan, weird as it may seem, words
forge links between us across distances
of time, space, and culture, the language
we share offering a spring we both can
drink from, though not get drunk on.
The new year, yes, is upon us, and
not to reciprocate your good wishes
and your loyalty would be unseemly. So
let us break some bread together in
your language I've made books in. Yes!
Can you believe it? Englishified I am
with a name I've earned, with the help
of many, including you, for which I'm
eternally grateful. The years of work
will pay off, for those of us who sally
forth into the brambles of ambition.
Expect the thorns of failure to flay
some skin, and the poison petals of
disappointment to engorge themselves
on the waters of hope. We must not
give in, though, but immunize ourselves
with good cheer to weather the neglect
that comes our way, regardless. How
we cope is sheer luck for some, dear
insight for others. I've had a taste
of both, for survival's boon I'll share
with you: Everything we do is a dare
to the gods who we know don't care."

'Wrecked nerves of a poet' (*from* Meta Frenz)

(their voices)

"Wrecked nerves of a poet on
skid row of the spirit—poverty's vow
taken seriously but not by the
world, we who judge and fault you
for crimes you haven't committed,
we who say the riches earned
are signs from god, omens from
fate while you remind us
like saints of old… and for
that we won't forgive you.
For in the world we see coming
you will be a derailed train of thought
we dare not get too near, for fear of
infection from the poor, don't you know?"

"Slowing it down, he's a downer
 in the eyes of the crowd."

"He's sowing seeds for the
 next round in human evolution?"

"Something like that. But very
 unorthodox. Nothing is what it seems."

"It never is."

"I mean, meaning included.
 It's relative in a larger, or
 deeper chaos, scientifically speaking."

"He keeps his rendezvous with destinies
 he thinks he has. It's how he lives."

"Jesus Christ, what a horror."

"More like a roar. From the abyss,
 to wake us up, or try to."

"He'll sacrifice his persona for his core."

"But knows the mask must be worn."

"Yes, that's called being born
 in his book. It slides off in death,
 the core to rejoin."

"In his realm, that's the coin
 he'll spend freely."

"How does he avoid bankruptcy"

"His means are modest,
 but not his aims.
 He has his sights on bigger fish."

"We wish! What a dish!"

"Yeah, a radar dish! He can hear
every word we're saying..."

"Holy shit!"

"Just sit tight, and watch. It's quite a show."

"A freak show?"

"He won't make it so. But we'll soon see."

"Japan has got him by the balls.
 Maybe that's what galls him."

"Or he limns the limits of his falls.
 That's what goads him."

"It's no show we've ever seen before."

"Nor perhaps again. Is there a Dr. Seuss
in the house?"

"He signals his travails
 but doesn't identify himself
 with them. Very detached,
 observing. Doesn't judge
 himself into corners and needless
 dilemmas. Yet still he's moral."

"To the core."

"No mean feat, especially when taking heat."

"No doubt about it. He's some treat."

"A Tweetie Bird of the Street."

Expatriate American Poet

(her voice)

"My my my he's got an I
softer than a kitten and
as wide awake as a lion.
A 'live' one on the other end
of this line. The thrill of the
chase is what I feel, and
he knows it, too. What I'll
say next will pull him in
closer before I'll let him
slip away, which I don't
want to happen too soon.
He's a fish for my fish story.
Let him stick around a little
while longer for a snapshot
of this sweet interlude. Quite
a dude, I'll say. He makes my day,
though it's nighttime already and
darker is where I'd lead him
if I could, but I can't. Oh well,
the hell with it. By the bell ringing
on my pussy's collar, he'll
know well what I mean. I mean,
what else is a poet for?
Ha-ha-ha-ha-ha-ha-hah!
The night breathes with him
in it, and it sighs, too.
Or do I hear myself through

his careful listening to
what I'm thinking and saying?
I'll give him a roll between
my legs for free, let him see
what he sees, then close
the deal and move on.
I've got other fish in my
'wide blue sea' and I don't
mean Okinawa! Ha-ha-ha-hah!

American Translator (*from* Meta Frenz)

(her voice)

"Pulled the thread that spreads wide our togetherness…
It's only developed in a few places, the silk.
My FB friend in Japan, pour some bourbon
on my face for starters, to show your tongue.
I'll unbutton your notions of power—
who's got it, who doesn't—in no time.
Concern yourself with me and learn
the pleasure of my displeasure, queen
of the bootsole you would look under
for the trace of precious Walt long gone.
Brace yourself, lover, for the unbuckling
tremor of truth only one's body knows for sure.
Everybody's staring at you, which empowers
you, don't you know? If you let it happen,
I'll take up philosophical positions a
thousand and one ways to hell and back
on my heavenly silk road. Come travel
with me and you'll see I offer no guarantee
but intellectual ecstasy rerouted through
our separate bodies and parts of the world.
Catch a glimpse of how to catch fire
and how to reach higher, glamour boy,
poet of mother's milk and father's silk.
You're of unique ilk and I'll circle you
like a moth a flame, you with no name!
Ha-ha-ha-ha-ha-hah!
Be my budding bud in Buddha's backyard.

Spirit, bitter is not better but you'll taste me
to the letter. (The husband looking over my shoulder
has got your number. Time to call it quits!)
Slave for me another time, me in my silky kimono
—aren't I sexy?

"About nothing you seem to know everything.
No, let me repeat that—what should I write?—
to wear you, foreigner, takes caution on your part.
Use art, you say, for social change? There's no chance
that dance will be danced here. Still, your spurt
is a stream I'll dip in and out of. With love, 'X'.
P.S. Son-wise, that is some shitty legacy, you'll
have to agree. And vulgar, too. This, my jab!"

Japanese College Students

—after summer *gasshuku* (camp)

"'Papa,' you're a hard player
to understand but your
smile lights up the
darkness for us and makes
us share in a happiness
we all feel with you. We
love the sight of you smiling
and laughing, and the good
time we had tonight we'll
never forget. Under the bridge
of stars, the river ran
cold and fresh, and you
waded into it fearlessly
with us, an act of bravery
and love we can only hope
to return someday. For
now we share the joy and
celebrate the summer days,
knowing as you must how
all too fleeting they are."

Expatriate American Professor

(his voice)

i

"Botsford has an eye for the girls but who
doesn't, for the thrills they offer the over-
the-hill gang I'm wholly part of. If it's
love what we do, do what we love, I'll
game him in my own fashion. It's what
I do, and do better than most. Best keep
my distance from our bloke of the cosmic
folklore. He's a fantasist that stays in play,
though, against all odds. Our gods will bill
him in advance, as they always do, for the
privilege (not right), to stay (not belong), on
turf Japonaise. It's no surprise he wants
to stick around. His lost-and-found routine
has balls galore which we keep tight against
our walls reminded, at least, of mending.

"The totality-tolls-for-thee scenario he
sketches in place is, at a glance, a failed
mad flight that has its sights dead set on
the dawn he'll never attain the heights of
if he goes on like he does, unlike the august
company he keeps in his mind's eye who
help steer him straight down the crooked
path he's on, a million miles in toto traversed,
were he worthy of the journey his heart

pines to make; instead he enters by this
treeline, now crossed, that reveals a world
he would win were he of courtly persuasion…
And the verdict's in--guilty by association!
High-mindedly he goes against the grain
of what flows rhythmically with him, out
of a conviction that the anti-road, the one
to ruin, leads backward to pearly salvation.
One would channel the anti-Christ himself, he
thinks, were one's ears, Dumbo-like, ready
to hear. But fear lays waste the power
to uphold the truth that holds time in place,
and oneself with it, in syncopated grace."

ii

"They're the Boss, I just do what's
expected of me, and I DO a lot. What
turnaround there be in our climate
doesn't make mates of us, but I'll
play the part without record fees
for now. Art's your racket, politics
is mine, and the twain don't meet.
Don't get me wrong, appreciation for
you galore, just limited by a door
few if any bother to walk through.
Who knew you'd last this long here,
severe weather conditions and all.
You're taller for not being small-minded
about so many walls we've put up.
Damn if you don't inspire awe
in the face of our awfulness. The gut
tells me you're no heart-robber

after all, but a winning combo of
the marathoner running in the pack and
a body-surfer sunning on the sand.
Time for you's an hour-glass of space
never run out of, trick-talk all we will."

Expatriate American (*from* Meta Frenz)

(his voice)

"Alan flabbergasted I was by you
and your radio station playing in
your head non-stop that we all
overheard and learned from, hearing
it shook our nerves and pelted our
sense of self—those waves of
electricity sizzling on a hotline
we couldn't get enough of yet feared
to know more about. Where, after
all, had self disappeared?
Sayonara-Sam-I-Am we called you,
wetting your pants in a cosmic dance.
We thought you silly, to be sure,
girly even. What did you get in return?
A cycle's worth of bad-mouthing
trash talk from the likes of me.

"What the cattle prodders do to earn
an honest day's wage is kill animals
fast, oh so fast not to ease their pain
but to get them as quickly as they can
to market. The market's the thing.

"Victim spared his victimhood and catches
the next wave. He moves quite loud
and tears up the dusty road behind him.
He's a free-wheeling poet with the nose

of a coyote and the guts of a rattlesnake.
I wouldn't put the money game past him,
I wouldn't put the name game past him,
the only game I'd put past him is
the shame game: he has none.

"You couldn't write a poem
to change my world, so there!
Squeezing the ounces out
of him will put me in the saddle.
Why else waste time and energy
on the flower stemmed in
waters of violence and bloodshed?
Who cares that he signs up for
the next passing wave. I'll have
what he's having, is NOT my motto.
A dim reminder of him in my memory
soon. Have a follow-up chat
and that's that. The starlit
front-pager stalls the years.
His rounds on the sly
won't keep him fly.
The indispensable, the
roundness, the white… Hmm,
changeling with a will of iron
does not a slave make… I'll see
his head rearing up to be
hammered back down again… Hmm,
may have other things on his mind."

American Editors

(their voices)

"He lights the heavens
we so rarely glimpse—
launching probes into
interstellar orbits."

"Stop bleeding, people.
He's on a splendid path
that wastes no ops
to plumb the depths
and scale the heights.
A poet's poet.
But manly.
He grieves, too,
being part of a world
that won't embrace him—
but that is his mission
he believes, he says,
and I believe him."

"He celebrates
anomaly and gives
it room to breathe."

"It's dizzying watching
him circle round and round
but he's no sideshow freak,
he's the main attraction

of what makes the soul
world go round, and his, too.
Very humble,
and humbling, too.”

“Let's see how far
we can redress injustice.”

“Finish tomorrow at 12:30.”

“Scale the heights no more?”

“No, build ladders for
readers to visit.
Abilities are not up to
his level, so it's time readers
were elevated.”

“Is it John Lennon calling
from the other side?”

“Seems that way. People
need to hear
what he has to say.
I'll dial him up
and see what he says.”

*

Life's tapestry,
in and out of love,
as Penelope knew,
which Odysseus

acted on, by
the arrow he let fly,
all twelve ax
handles perfectly
shot through,
while Telemachus, waiting
for his day, dreams
the night away.

American Translator

(his voice)

i

"Alan, there's nothing smarmy about his
army of love. His weapon of choice is
telling it like it is, up front and in your
face, all subtleties included, nuanced
into higher realms without losing one
iota of the energies available to him in
the lower realms. It's a hard row to hoe
and his harm, though not technically
self-induced, runs dangerously close
to being so. Still, the voice is remarkably
astute, it's heady stuff all around, as
'T'-san said. I wonder how he survives
at the classroom level, if not at the *kaigi*
level. He has risked everything—his health,
his job, his reputation—by going down this
path. Whatever awaits him, the question
must be asked—Is it worth it? The answer,
it seems, as I was able to glean today, is
an affirming, undeniable, whole-hearted
Yes: there's no turning back for this poet.
I only hope he grows the necessary cajones
for what he must endure. Meanwhile
keep faith with him we must, and will."

ii

"Alan now mines the far-flung
into the close-knit, an epic sung
to the tune of cosmic, and I among
the voices he hears, a cacophony rung
from the cold and desolate universe
we each inhabit, separate, alone,
the 'American way' and all that.
What he will have found in verse
is more than Japanese, is a star shone
high in the sky the gods will have begat
for the said poet's *Weltanschauung*.
But let him know the foreign tongue
as I have—as the old eating the young.
Poetry, for me, is no plaything."

Japanophiles

They go over the same ground
again and again called transience—
the clear demarcation of sound
advice, were they giving it, sense
made from Oriental, or Eastern,
or Asiatic mysteries lightly worn
on a kimono sleeve for all to see,
the *wabi sabi* version of beauty,
the cracked ceramic bowl held
in reverence embodying a world
the tea masters fought to preserve,
its rustic simplicity, less-is-more curve
of learning which, I confess, I'd aspire
to stay on but for losses that conspire
to add up, leaving me with nothingness
that, admit it, passes for Zen happiness.
Still, Japanophiles who are savvy
won't openly trash Western culture, it's tacky
and weeb-like, and besides, they know,
I'm sure, a Pinot Noir from a Bordeaux,
and relish the aesthetic points
scored from downing British pints
in a bar where darkness covers everything,
even, yes, this Scorpion's sting.

Japanese Support Staff

(their voices)

i

"The monk in our midst makes mincemeat
of his enemies, and he has many, mean-spirited
ones aplenty, whom he appears not to give
a second thought to of late, unlike last
year when his feet, if not tied, were held to
the fire. In dire straits he was—hospitalization,
surgery, the works. He milked our goodwill
but good, and strives to re-earn the same
on what he knows now will be our turf till
kingdom come. The trouble with his ilk,
however, is that the kingdom comes,
whether early or late, in every passing
moment. It's a view he pays a steep
price for, act nice all he will…"

ii

"He's lovely, tall and handsome
and small where it counts—the ego
where the West thinks it's best.
The tales he tells, I hear,
are surrender personified, for
a new person and its ride to glory.
But I bet it's lonely, so I'll give him
a warm look that, for all he knows,
is a hook in the waters I swim."

iii

"I'm a beaut in a suit. I adore
his gaze, and the ways
he shoots from the hip I swivel
for his eyes only. Lord he's a
he-man for my time. Let him rhyme
me by his tongue, then
we'll have a song truly sung
from east to west and back again.

"European-Italian blood this bud's
coursing with, too, not only
Anglo-Saxon brains. Jewish passion
in his veins rallies us to his cause.
We've swiftboated him enough.
He's shown us he's got the stuff.
What's the use going on, when he's
got the juice? Bots doesn't botch
things up, as scotch and water
does. He's got buzz.

"No use looking for an op
to raid his fridge. What for?
Nothing he's got is frozen!
His mind leaps to no conclusions.
He's bagged a winner with his first
shot. For him I'll go out and shout."

iv

"You come in here tall and small—
how do you do that, sensei, all

wide-eyed you are, while wondering
we are at the wanderer in our midst.
I miss knowing you better,
but no one really does—know you,
that is—so it's down to compromise
and a shot of your mojo-eyed
goodness we stand in front of,
bathing in its boyishness and
handsome manliness, too. Who
you are, poet, stars in our moment's
heaven and, darling, you shine.
A fantasist you make me, in a flash!
An aching desire I won't put down
or out, like a fire you spread.
What hair falls into, cupped and full,
are hands you can stroke me by,
for minutes or hours, it's your call,
like this yarn we've wound into a poetic ball."

Japanese College Student

(her voice)

i

"Sensei bends his ear my way and my body
shudders at the thought of him listening.
Here I am where *we* are, such is his star
in my sky, though heavenly reward must
be earned, not learned, so onward we go.
What we know we'll share en route, all
the way down to the roots of the tree
some call cosmic, keeping track of what
we find. Mr. Alan has the eyes of a cat
in heat, or is that me mirrored in his eyes
where we meet? Either way, the hay we
make today goes a long way in staying
the course, the one I'm taking with you,
sensei, and the one we're both on. Bone
and flesh in knowledge of love, revivifies
like Lazarus the guarded heart turned stone."

ii

"This is *my* love story, Alan, and
don't you forget it! Step by step,
chapter by chapter, we're getting
to the love story of my dreams—
my heart is a different matter.
My mind's made up as to how

the story unwinds, but slowly
we must go, lest it come undone
and unravel before it's time.
No need for us to rhyme, no
need for us to chime—the love
part you call 'art' is what this
is, the woman's artfulness, which
the man knows not even the half of—
think what you will. Step by step
the path unfurls, one foot in front
of the other, where the path turns
visible on a dime, invisible just in time…
We heart your art but it's only
a part of what's coming ahead
or behind and that's the part
the whole of which equals the
whole that is an art unseen as
it is seen by the human heart,
the choices we make in seeing
and the voices that remake each scene,
word by word, world by world,
in what others call the inner life,
is hidden from overt sight yet as real.
Let the feelings reunite us to
what has no bottom line, symbols
colliding to embrace the next sign."

iii

"Your 'touch' is a torch I
own, so better watch out,
'cause Santa—that's me—is
coming to town and will

clean up, leaving you without
a cent to your name…
Though the trail I'm on
leads by bitter scent to
the bulge in your pocket.
Yeah, we both know Rocket
Man likes his fuel, no
fool he… Gal pal you'd
play with you'd pay for, too,
and I mean through the noze,
scent and all. Heaven-sent
I may be, but hell-bent, baby,
is what I am. Can't touch this,
Teach. I'd outwit imagination's
reach every time, Einstein be damned."

iv

"Golden drop smashes the brainy conceit
of his wonderment. Who knows who he'd be
if he weren't a prof at our uni? What makes him
imagine the world's a better place for his having
written poems about it, or different in any way from
what it still is and always has been: a scar, a torn
heart, a cut thread, a bespattered cloth—all heaped
at his poetic doorstep if he wants it? We'll graze
his daisy field and dance until his jig is up.
We know better than to fall for the fallow pasture
he has on offer. Praising Christ doesn't mean
we should be raised on him. For different folks,
are different spokes of the wheel tradition spins."

Faculty Meeting (1)

"It's a new day and new way to greet
the meeting we have to hold, no bold
moves but careful detachment from
earlier attachments while staying reciprical
and maintaining cordial relations.
Today's order of business is continuity.
No, nothing new, beyond, yes, what we
have to do. And that, once again, is plenty.
Sailing right along, we won't keep you long
if we can help it. But listen close.
A dose of togetherness goes a long way.
Don't underestimate a table for being square.
We know where we all sit, or stand, and
while fence-sitting is tolerated, even encouraged,
think of what's lost with the sixth sense
left out or shelved for the duration.

"Force contained by force is, of course,
one option. But secretive is the nature
of the beast here, so open combat is
rarely engaged in. We keep it clean,
taking satisfaction in no holds barred
indirection, left right out in
the open, close or far from cries of war,
the curse of siblings close-quartered and
wanting more space in the time remaining them.
Home, or its equivalent, expands and contracts
accordingly, communally, spiritually, rhythmically,
a message embedded in, of all things, the origin

of beauty, rebellious or not, that loved and
fought for, becomes embellished when died for.

"He's all over the place mapping an
imagination that pursues him, as
words of prey."

Faculty Meeting (2)

"I, for one, am enamored of his name
that nobody knows. It fits him nobly,
and embodies his modesty."

"Too small his name, too big his aim,
that's what I think. Nothing's going
to change my mind. It's a hit or miss
affair I won't indulge. His spirit tickles us
into laughing at our own banality.
What self-respecting evil allows that?"

"It's what's allowable now that becomes
inevitable later, which is unacceptable!"

"The peripatetic knife blade speaks
for us all. God almighty, he's made of steel!"

"Discover with him vistas you never
knew existed. Then be glad you're
not him. A sad but true story
brought to you on his whim.
A king cut from unkingly cloth.
I'll admire his tailor, but we're still Boss!"

"Inspiration turned on like a fountain
now spurts, now gushes forth like prophecy.
How do we shut him off?!"

"Notice on the other side of his door,

you eat chicken on the floor."

"But that's illogical and unclean".

"That's not as illogical as it may seem."

"I've balled him, and soiled him,
and left him in a gutter, and
still he treats me with kindness
and respect. It's horrendous
guilt I feel, that I may never get over."

"It's too brilliant even for the
best of us. Unbelievable!"

"I can tell you, though, all the pies
you can stuff your faces with won't
make this clown less of a circus!
The high-wire act he pulls off at
our expense leaves us all gasping,
but then what? His ingenuity runs
out even on him! Back to zero we
all go. What a show!"

"Time to bow knowingly and move on.
Words he doesn't understand, go unheard."

American Translator

(his voice)

"We plow fields for future yields, is my battle plan,
history bringing up the flank in every maneuver.
That's how wars are fought in these and other
domains, modern accoutrements notwithstanding,
though it does nobody any good to openly admit it.
The territory we gain by inches is for flag-planting
the self's name for fame, worth all the sacrifices
and then some. Home grows wider in the process."

(their voices)

"Alan has his head
in the clouds, while
the crowds below honor
his heartfelt honesty, or
would if they read him.

"Public validation goes a long way
when at times you're hanging
by a thread."

"If you hold onto the female
and let the male go,
energies that weren't there
before now come into play
that are neither male nor female,
as eye-opening as it is mysterious!"

"Climbs the summit of life
while threading the needle
of death—a terrifying paradox."

"Honors what the imagination can do
when organized religion is through,
while hinting at possibilities
as breathtaking as they are new."

"Excitement he brings to the page
will do wonders for the age."

"Without arresting Time as arrow,
he releases Time as circle.
What we can learn from this
frees us to learn even more,
a never-ending story within a story!"

Super Sento Spa Counter Clerk

(her voice)

"He shows true feeling and who am I
not to reciprocate and look into the eyes
he sees by, to see wonders reflected there
momentarily, those mild demonstrations
of human facts that harden or soften
according to their viewer at one with the view:
For the Westerner's haunted sight, jewels
that lay unplucked from night's diadem
are trivial pasttimes shared only in passing,
or are souvenirs exchanged upon one's return.
East or west, he knows either way the road leads
the same, twin vistas the shoreline reveals
where ships of sleep and ships of waking ply
the waters, vanishing wave upon wave like the bow
releasing the arrow through time where its truer
target, the future, for our sakes is born."

Cave Canem

— *New York Times* interview, Nov. 27, 2023

(their voices)

"Your body against
the concept of no morality."

"Smile for the camera of life
is our panacea for
the relentlessness of strife."

"The victory is not in awards
but in our survival."

"No matter how justified,
there's no defense for
the prosecution of war."

"Oh, absolutely.
I think creativity
is a forest you find paths
in and out of."

"Time allots us space
to experience eternity
in small doses."

"I'd much rather tune in
to the end of the witch."

"Corralled into doing something
he's ill-fitted for, the poet
fulfills his promise while
champing at the bit."

"America is going ahead
to where we're gonna
practice what we preach."

"The bell thing really
tells you a lot,
how hell resounds
in the ears of heaven."

"To retrieve what's lost,
ignore the cost
of embracing the rest."

"It's funny.
But it's mistakenly funny."

"Race to immortality
wears you out, so then
you can barely be seen."

Yoko Ono

Japanese multimedia artist and singer

i

She dared to make music in John's wake,
on and on a star-crossed lover for life,
season now of glass, now of grass, a promise
kept even as she wept, New York flow she
entered and would never leave, spiritually,
poet in her own right, art-maker, heart-shaker,
a voice echoing room to room from the Dakota
to a grateful generation and beyond, glory be
to the mother of the universe, she would sing,
bloodstain on John's eyeglasses preserved forever.

ii

Yoko Ono and Sinead O'Connor:
the former used peace and love
as her defiance, insisting we
come together; the latter
used truth and rage as her defiance,
damning the tyrannies
allowed to go scot-free.

iii 'Amaterasu'

She withdraws into her cave
for inspiration, and listens to

her heartbeat, the waves
splashing on the shore peace-
fully, compassion for you
and me its abiding magnificence,
the journey not forsworn,
though the long night forlorn,
now standing outside the entrance,
her destination the morning
sunrise, her power adorning
so many suns whirled
about a centerless world.

Japanese Poet

(her voice)

"Felt always loved,
but what good is a 'good guy'
if he's eaten up alive? One less
guy, I guess, good or bad, to
mess up this worsening world.

…

"Alan snap out of it!
We'll not go over this ledge
in my lifetime. Of rhyming, beware!
Silliness prevails in make-believe
worlds unless the reality principle
is adhered to. What is that? It's what's
coming around every corner in my
field of vision, that's what. But as Eliot
once said: Humankind cannot bear much
reality. Or as Walt wondered: Is identity
beyond the grave a beautiful fable only?
I can't or won't answer for you, but if we both
belong to this reality we're creating here, as
much as we're inhabiting it, than I say good
luck comes in threes: body once,
spirit twice, soul thrice—whatever that
means! It's the only recipe you'll get
out of me. Did you think the gods
would desert the summit willingly?

Yes, the naked eye can see as much
if not more than any third-eye you throw
our way, no matter how deep you think you go.
No depths that sleep reaches can equal
the appearances I've gleaned on
the surface of things, ten-thousand and counting…
The Tanikawa's of the world reign, I'm afraid,
supreme, so my breath will not imbue
a future unchanged but will, by a husband-
and-wife way, realign alliances to afford
newer resources we can invest in later.
Watchful we must remain, I admit, of
getting nailed. It's their domain, and they know it.
Sleep in it for a moment and you'll die.
Here the names we go by, no
matter how poetical, won't add up
to much except an 'I' that, with us or
against us, brings no pie in the sky.

"So get a grip. And keep yourself
together. Don't let your core fly away
or soar upwards toward the sun…
Stop mooning us from where you stand
inside your door. We'll welcome you, but
only so far as the shores where the waves
hit the sand by the light of the moon.
See ya soon!…

"…The goofy guy who once was sly
I've got to keep my eye on. Who knows
where he'll go next? He's certainly not shy."

*

"One is in love with them
every moment they're on screen."

"Joseph's coat of many colors now in ruins."

"No. Just in repairs."

"Is there no end to this?"

"Honey, time makes space redemptive.
Welcome to the hardened imagination."

"In heaven's name
without hell's fame!"

"Should she ever be sick, scatter
flower petals across her hospital bed."

"Wither the new world coming?"

A (Brief) Homage to American Poetry

In the middle of the night, america,
you appear to my sight. Longingly
I wonder if there's light enough
to return to you, and might
I stay in your mirroring sight
through these words I write,
cross my heart hope to die
never having to say goodbye.

*

"Presenting a Western mindset
in a Japanese context, the poet
is registering the effects of the culture
on his psyche… It is to Japan
of the mythic mind,
of Amaterasu in all her glory,
that he welcomes the reader."

And, smiling, there she was.

i Emily Dickinson

(letter)

"The work we do, wording
and unwording grief's sentence.

"Such is our pain
in front of the world's
peering eyes, a vouchsafing
of its magnitude,
and replenishment, too."

*

Mystery and history
are secondary places.

We have Emily typing
in the background.
Please be present.

Sue signaled abortion
in those years.

    What does it mean to have a self,
    to dwell in possibility?

    The democrat
    in a piss pot.

    The monarch
    marks the spot.

*

"I weathered the brainstorms
of God. Among all the synapses
firing I managed to hold my own,
hunkered down for the duration.

"I shall simultaneously
assert and refute
the absurdity of God.
The cosmic world
in his place
is more than enough.

"That we can change the world
through language, I'm not sure about.
What I am certain of, though, is
that language can cause the
greatest changes in us."

*

For her, poetry was a calling, not a career.
She simply wanted no part of the hustle…

"The marketplace that is home to me,
where evening and morning vie
for the hand of eternity."

ii Ralph Waldo Emerson

No one was as alien to churches as Emerson.
Yet, soft-spoken, he was hard-pressed
to define experience in any
terms other than spiritual.
For him, life of the spirit
gave birth to experience.

Emerson begins "Experience" with the question:
"Where do we find ourselves?"
In language we dwell. Language is the house
or temple of being. We dwell there,
in our highest capacity, *poetically*.
What the poet's doing is steering people
to a self that goes higher and higher
by way of transmissions, or possessions
of spirit…

iii Walt Whitman

Taste the leaves
of grass on
your tongue.

Here is where the celebratory I
meets the self-effacing I.

By way of the optative voice his persona
constitutes a posthumous image.

  Whitman's fraternal utopia, his America
  of readers as brothers and sisters. But what happens
  when the brothers start killing each other?
  What happens when there's civil war?

Indeed, the beginning of the war
would mark the end of his bohemian days
and set him on another, more purposeful course.

Walt Whitman chief of the local
doctors who got around in the hospitals.

We bow to the sacrifices
 he willingly made for others.

Whitman created his afterlife,
his so-called immortality,
while his bones otherwise
rest undisturbed.

Isn't it odd
how the classic work
—no matter how old—
stays perennially *present*.
Or, rather, allows us to stay
within its *presence*
for the sake of making
new meanings.

Wait Whitman—
the son also rises.

iv H.D.

What's been shared over time
forms the basis of
more or less than time.
But still, needing spin.

v Stanley Kunitz

"Kunitz… how, I wonder, did he gain ascendancy
in the ranks of contemporary poets?"

"When he became worthy of notice,
history came calling."

*

He lived to a hundred,
the mustachioed poet,
writing his way
through the layers, poetry
as it was called, for wholeness's
sake, dissections notwithstanding,
the years accumulating from the other
side which he courted
and eventually wedded, by will
and wonder, whose mythic lines
were woven into work he lived for,
played out in secret gardens
day in and day out on night's loom,
while rapture and grace, doom and dread informed
his steps, the path forward into memory,
passing through changes, losses
in getting there.

vi Franz Wright

The day after he died he came to me
in a dream and spoke, saying things I didn't
necessarily want to hear, let alone
understand. But the words, fresh

and exacting as his poems, rose up
to greet me, grounded in feeling
I couldn't ignore.
I wrote them down in my dream
journal where his voice, to this day,
reverberates with that fierce haranguing tone
of a prophet of (conflicted) love
and grief, doomed to go unheard
save in a dream.

vii Mary Oliver

She veers into cringe territory
occasionally, when we, reading,
least expect it, her life-enhancing
stories worth the hiccups, sublime
revels in prose that are pleasures
she offers in their veering, endearing
us to her even more. And why not?
She may have lost her edge with age
but she harvested the banner years
she spent in the depths of her imagination,
content to live out her remaining years
now in undying 'devotions.'

viii Forrest Gander and Jack Gilbert

—after their interview "Owning Yourself"

On the mountain of their desires, they scaled
the heights and beheld the vistas that rolled on

into the language that poetry took them to, walled
no more but opened now in every direction
that words could register, their voices ribald
and serious, sounding secrets in succession,
before descending again, energized, told.

ix a deceased poet

The click of the pen, the wit
of the mind at work, the pit
of the stomach aroused by
her poetic compassion on the fly,
the truth of her words, their
accuracies, and breaths of air,
now the sorrow at her passing,
but not without her having sung
the roiling depths of her years.

x a haunted poet

This is America's haunted
man, in his seventies now,
veteran of the cursed war he carries
with him, alone with his thoughts.
This is America's wounded
soldier consumed with rage
and regret, but neither without
a poet's touch burnishing both.
This is America's forlorn
lover mirroring, sure-footed, a heart
shattered by the words it hears,

one lone beat at a time.

xi Louise Gluck

—after *Proofs & Theories*

(her voice)

"My husband guides my hand as I
write this, sentences forging a way
out of the fog of bewilderment into
the passion of clarity. I have been wounded
into this syntax, thrown off the wound's
paralysis, to make a healing effort
in language that solves nothing, resolves
everything in its paradoxes, its otherness,
its mastery above all. With this song, I thee wed."

—after *Poems, 1962-2012*

The journey intact, with detours galore,
you have wandered far
into a bewilderment that autumnal
music repairs note by note,
the mourning dove in the garden lifting
off into a song of her own, fluttering,
fluttering, the cicadas singing along.
Cool cumulus climbs the sky into
an atmosphere charged with fears
overcome, the dew on the grass confirms.
Houses sit on their foundations for
the winter ahead, where the crickets

at night, singing being, will have gone.
Not yet nine o'clock, the morning beckons,
the book in your lap heavy and slow
with undoing upon undoing you know, their
poisons seeping past words into anguish untold,
dust emptying into a broken hour of thanks,
writing the bones whose weight you adore.

xii Jorie Graham

—after "Day" (her voice)

"We make room for
the distance in us
that, when traversed, brings
us back to where we began
to sing, for the time we had
to spend on earth was being
lost to us even as we woke
to our bitter reckoning, if
you could call it that, the day
all we ever had to work
out our resemblances to each
other, were we capable of seeing
and hearing those nearnesses
that the heart beats for, night's
rhythmic salutations from the timeless
we sought to make real,
our day in a house of feel."

—after the *Rumpus* Interview (her voice)

"Time has morphed for me into a futureless
horizon that attention is built for and imagination
is embracing as we live our days and nights,
but there is no time to speak for others,
I can only speak for myself as I go forward
trying to preserve my humanity in the face
of eventual extinction, my own and humanity's,
if things don't radically change for us, a nightmare
I cannot wake from in the waning days of my life."

—after an interview w/ Katy Waldman, 2023 (her voice)

"Sorry, you're losing my thought…
now… Incantatory Poetics is what I would call
my operating system, so to speak, one
that sends radio waves out for readers
to catch and in turn transmit into action,
for if words cannot propel readers into
action then they are nothing more than
inert matter, dead weight in the universe,
but if they pulse with life, if language lives
in the heights and depths then it can radiate
in all directions signaling to future generations
our existence here on earth was not without meaning,
not without moral outrage, not without love for
the earth and all its inhabitants, so, we poets
who measure our success by short-term gains are
doomed to fail, but allowing for the long view puts one
in a position of strength, positing a changed, or
hoped-for, future as not only desirable but attainable,
and it's to this future I give what time and attention
I have left in me."

xiii Patti Smith

(her voice)

"I don't cherish the memory so much
as the reality of my friends who lived
and died refusing conventions, embracing
their gifts with gusto and panache, the sight
of them in my mind's eye offering delight
in my later years, half-waiting for my postscript,
my final release from the worldly coil."

xiv a mindfulness poet

He's tall, wears a hat, teaches
mindfulness, and bludgeons us
with his charms, egolessness his aim
he knows he falls short of,
sadness cascading down
with each new line of thought pursued
to its inevitable end, 'here and now'
a haphazard way of saying
it never stops, human follies and
weaknesses the real show
after all, say what we will,
counting among his friends the everything
and all he stays true to,
come what may, honesty being
the best line of defense against
the illusions he'd cling to
as a vine to a tree,
or a poet his poetry.

xv an acclaimed poet

They all sound alike, his poems,
with the voice poets regard so highly,
his own, one he likes the sound of,
and is respected and admired for
…but what of the voices channeled, each
with a tone unique, vocabulary singular,
registers varying, a cacophony
of the Many subliminally emitted
into an orderly chaos, a momentary chorus,
not espousing an 'exemplary' anything
but the writing them, a matter of sheer survival.

xvi Diane Seuss

Objectivity is the object
lesson she would teach us
is all about
love, if we could,
if we would,
bear it,
as the subject
at hand.

xvii Dorianne Laux

—after *Life on Earth*

She's the moon she swoons over
and swims in, its light buoying

her up and back, back to her past
no darkness will overshadow,
if she has any say in the matter,
her words on the page a sun-
lit terrain where she, Earth, shines on.

Seven Arts + 1

i Caedmon

   first English poet (his voice)

"To speak in the bone-still air
we hatch a forked prayer:
say the words for where
the night is long and has a song
for you to hear, lend it your ear,
fear not the dark hour its power,
the pale rider's charging hooves
bearing down past the flower
of the moon, where soon
memory, kept alive,
lights the shadow behind the grave:
this the reason, of this season."

ii Vincent van Gogh

   Dutch painter (his voice)

"I am not who I would have been
had I not discovered the various colors
of the world, saturating each scene
with their light and shadow, the real
work of time and change."

iii James Joyce

    Irish novelist

'Does nobody understand?'
Joyce supposedly said
on his death bed,
the last words heard before
slipping away
into the land of the dead.

iv Keith Jarrett

    American pianist & composer (his voice)

"High notes or low, improvisation takes me where
the music runs through my heart to chords in air."

v David Cronenberg

    Canadian film director

The climactic scene of any life
as the moment not of staring into
the abyss but of climbing out of it
to render the 'to be or not to be'
moot, defines his films in the end,
his compulsion to tell the body's
stories notwithstanding, for he
searches the entrails of his mind
for a reason for being, the terrors
of death-in-life rendering the plot

shocking and nightmarish, filled
with gore whose details he relishes
to the extreme, an auteur of horror
that would make Poe proud.

vi Makoto Shinkai

    Japanese filmmaker (his voice)

—after *Your Name*

"We have traversed the cosmos
to find each other, yet no proof
was given us outside the heart
we felt the other with, magic
commingling our lives were made for.
How many times our paths crossed
without the eye of the soul confirming it,
later realizing missed chances, broken
rendezvous's we had to fight our way
back from, to link our lives once more."

vii Peter O'Toole

    English actor (his voice)

—after an interview re: *Lawrence of Arabia,* dir. David Lean

"The eye of the needle threaded
with love and ambition opens
the universe entire, with never

a regret for the losses entailed,
and when the time comes to look
back, one sees one's life deeply
lived go on and on and on forever."

viii Annie Dillard

American writer

She absconds with the goods of mystery's
questions asked pointedly, with no need of
answers. Or those, at least, definitive in nature.
She leaves a trail for us to follow, however.
She knows where she has been better than
where she is going. That is the fun of it.
She knocks down idols along the way.
Others she comes into contact with come
in for a hammering of sorts, her jokey meta-
physical love of the cracking one-liner that,
presto! turns us inside out, butt-naked as
a newborn. She smiles at us under the sun—
hers—with her blazing, scintillating lines.

Cody-Rose Clevidence

American poet

--after "from 'This Household of Earthly Nature; an Essay'"
2023

(their voice)

"We need to take the discussion
outside, hereafter loneliness
will confine itself to the universe
I am nothing
more than you,
so, let's agree
to disagree
I'm going to confiscate
you from the poetic
landscape and put
my mother in instead
where the joke's on her

"How can you be alive
here, with me,
I ask you
and like the music of
the spheres nothing
is ever the same again
Is not that good enough
for us, I'll wager it is

"There's a nice person
out there
I can feel him
He's reading my poem
as we speak
That's a coincidence
and then there's beauty

"The cake I bake
with a file in it
will serve a purpose after all
I'm trying to get through that
period, the laws
of water apply, scaled to rhyme

"You who have given so much
of your time, thank you
We bow and move on
not to greener pastures
but to bluer ones

"He's going to hurt you
into a hundred little pieces
so, I'd advise against it,
inviting him into your poem

"There are others, so many others
who will rebuild your poem
and not hang you out to dry

"That building was strange
better to enter it
and leave it

as you please,
you hear them say

"And that's
what they do"

'Honor thy fathers' (*from* Meta Frenz)

(their voices)

"They're great
at what they do."

"Fair weather, foul weather
foolproof friend. Then they're
pretty good men, who put the screens on."

"Oh yeah. This might be a satellite dish."

"How do you know what he's thinking?"

"You don't, you put up a smokescreen
and hope for the best.
Can put Renaissance at the helm."

"Hideaway Island for sure.
He's indefatigable."

"I'm tired. Let's go to bed."

"Honor thy fathers
with patronage of the soul,
it seems. Sure works for him.
But a lie others make of it, or have to.
Too much is at stake if going
forward this way. And he knows it, too.
He has no beef with the bounty-hunting

called history. The free-for-all of the soul
is where he plants his flag. Unfortunately
no one can see it flying there. A banner
at daybreak indeed."

"Will he sue to get heard?"

"Why bother if he gives away
the profits? Nice meeting him, though,
on turf he calls spiritual. It's a ghostly
affair that gets him everywhere
but the top of anyone's reading list.
It's no con he perpetuates, either.
The magic is real in his book.
Extraordinary for a tiger with no stripes.
Seals the deal on every page.
It's no kiss and tell
but what a trip to hell!
Angels of his better nature
gave proof through the night
and won the day, it looks like.
A roundabout wiz of U.S. Route 66 kind.
It's an open road he won't bail on:
try higher self on the continental shelf.
Lies or no lies, he picks his battles
and goes forth, a knight's errand
or a fool's, either way.

"His slice of lies is a whole lot of
pie in the face of Father Time,
for it's an open space he welcomes
at all costs, including the cost to him.
It makes for thrillingly tall tales

at the outer limits of the twilight zone
he calls imagination, but I call Goofy
Two-Shoes Goes to Town. But hey,
live wire honors the energy coursing
through him in a wholly original way—
Say it ain't so, Joe meets
Marilyn Monroe's diamonds…"

*

Swinger on the boughs
of poetry, be
grounded fearlessly in
the vacuum where
air of discovery rushes in
and hold on for
your dear, dear life.
He toiled and labored in obscurity
for the oblivion that awaited him
is a description that fits
nearly all of us. How ashamed I feel
trying to put my name *out there*,
how small my ambition comes to seem.
Rather, let imagination invoke
its ten thousand names *in here,* where it rings
heartily to the bell-sound of love.

Haruki Murakami & Hayao Kawai

Japanese novelist (his voice) talking with Japanese psychologist

—after *Haruki Murakami Goes to Meet Hayao Kawai*

"I have drowned in English and have resurfaced
in Japanese, and this is why translation from
one language to another inspires in me the need
to tell my story, not in any logical sequence,
mind you, but in a fantasy-like progression
that dreams reflect or imagination embodies,
a progression outside the bounds of time per se,
but that space contains in a way that images
allow, call it a flow if you will, arising from
depths that language taps into, whether in English
or in Japanese, where structurally speaking
images constitute the weight and breadth and height
of the language and the writer must follow where
these core elements lead, regardless of one's intention.
I focus, in other words, on the flow of the language
and its images rather than on the events of the plot.
In this way I have the maximum of freedom to create
the world I find within myself, with a minimum of rules
to obey, and in this way the process gives me my story-
line across both languages, the overlapping sense
of identity I feel being the true story getting itself told.

"The stories I, as it were, dig wells in myself to find
lead back out into the world in unforeseen ways.
That's why I need physical strength in order

to write, the mind working in tandem with the body
is a necessity without which I could not dig the wells,
nor pass through walls. The body's logic plays its part
for cumulative effects that transcend the human ego.
I'd like to think of it as 'teaness' reigning supreme
over the likes of coffee. Besides, no matter what
I say or do, I'd rather be fed by a woman.

"As regards the past, we as Japanese have not faced
it and are doomed therefore to cater to history's
violence, internalize it and inflict it upon others
unless channeled in new ways, verbalized in my case,
which is extremely difficult, but for the sake of
healing, necessary, and I'll go on writing to achieve it."

Chris Rock

American comedian

—after a Netflix show, 2023 (his voice)

"…Slaves, niggahood...
I'se climbing
I see the mountaintop
and from where I'm at,
it's reachable!

"Powerful end hook
with a drop the mic moment.

"It's about dreams
and reading the signs too much.

"It may be something to think
about, drear!

"Living in a partial place
It may be just me
but it may be something
to think about, drear.

"Humor still got legs, motherf-cker!
We're rising, like I said.
The mountaintop is near
I can see it.

"That's right brothers and sisters
I'm keeping it real
Scattershot, maybe, but real.

"That's right! Whities…
who needs 'em?
Got 'em in our sights
keeping it real.

"But mirroring's what we do.

"We've got our f-ckin' knives,
who needs guns?
We're slicing and dicing this shit!

"The paper cuts hurt the most.

"When you're walkin' in the dark,
any light is better than none.

"If you like it so much,
I'll put it in your bag!

"That's right. I'm seeing
the mountaintop,
and it's rich!

"If it's holy you want,
say a prayer for me!

"That's right, adversity
is travelin' so fast,
diversity don't know

what hit 'em!

"Shut the f-ck up!
It's me you're talkin' to!
Bedrock mayhem.
Over and out."

Nicholas Cage

American actor

—after *The New Yorker* interview, July 8, 2024 (his voice)

"The white world I'm part of
doesn't know me from Adam
is how I'd like it to be if I had
my druthers. Meanwhile, the
ranting and raving parts of
films I've acted in get memed
as the 'real me,' which is far
from being the real me as
I can imagine. But that's what
you get on the Internet these
days, a mountain out of a
molehill, where mystery comes
a distant second if at all, the
not knowing being the real
truth of an actor, that is *moi*,
who I prefer the public not
to know too much about
celeb-wise. Give me the artist
any day, say, for this interview,
artistic license activated in
the here and now for the white
world who'll read it, but the
non-white world will know me
a lot better, don't ask me how,
it is what it is. Trust me, they know."

'The news brings news from the other'

The news brings news from the other
end of supposition: suppose you weren't
doing this but doing *that*, suppose you
aren't who you are but are the *other*
you're not? This bangs on the door
of desire reality calls high-mindedness,
but for the lowdown you have a heart
you open and, knock-knock, pumps
out the beat you walk on called your life.
It's new news wherever you are or may be.

The social network game ruses the news
with players who've won the day at night's
expense. It's no go for moonwalkers like
yourself. Making hay while the sun shines
won't unbury the dead where they plumb
the depths of misery, corruption, and mayhem.
Christ himself couldn't walk on those waters
where the arc of civilization goes to drown.
Anyone with a lifeline swims to a farther
shore of belief, one that idols won't be built on
save for an idyll of a would-be poet who, early
or late, sings for his supper meant to last.

'The percentage of poetry' (*from* Meta Frenz)

(their voices)

"The percentage of poetry
not being read grows slim,
for the poet's way we owe to him
and his psychobabble."

"It's hot enough to turn
grey fifty shades!"

"How long before he'll take
the hint?
His way against ours
costs him a mint."

"He knows that the universe right
under his nose can be seen
360 degrees if he slows. So he does."

"Stop thinking my thoughts!
Who do you think you are?"

"I have plenty more where
these come from."

"Where do they come from?"

"I wish I knew."

"So do I."

"Bye."

"Bye."

"No, it doesn't work."

"It works."

"She had a huge illness."

"You have to be extra sensitive."

"Whose thoughts are these?"

"They're mine."

"No, they're mine!"

"Who are you?"

"I'm not you, that's for sure."

"Speech was planted in my brain."

"A hard rain's gonna fall, one drop at a time."

"I'm telling you, we all
live in a yellow submarine.
In the end, I'll come out."

"Fosters awareness in the pink

undersides of things."

"Aromatherapy might do the trick."

"Close your eyes. He'll hex your brain."

"I don't have time for this."

"My wants are immaterial.
It's his that count."

"Craver for attention he's not.
Showman of a stellar kind."

"Some excellent advice—
treat your customer with respect;
every day's a new day;
and nothing's over till it's over.
What's to argue with that?"

"Capture the flag some other day."

"Absent me."

Joseph Brodsky

after the video 'Joseph Brodsky: A Maddening Space' (1990)

i

His talent pulled him forward into
spaces more maddening than he thought
possible, the shored up ruins left
behind for the living stream un-
blocked by either hope or despair,
a procession, if you will, he would
one day be part of, but not yet, his
getting his feet wet all the proof
he needed of that particular pudding.

ii (his voice)

"I don't venerate heroes, the 'shock
treatment' at the 'hotels' they put
me in having disabused me of, well,
those outdated notions. Heroism's
for the birds, so to speak. More
interesting, I think, is to honor
a poet's resources, such as they are,
which allow him or her to keep
writing in the face of not being
read, or of being read too much,
as the case may be. Perfecting one's
talent at whatever cost to oneself,
is the only yardstick a poet has,
the bread of the crumbs, yah?...

"They're just guys like us,
you and I sitting here talking,
trying to round out a picture one
can live with, or maybe live for.
That, in essence, is all the heroism
I'd need among the many people
I've known, living or dead, the poet's
voice, mind you, the last to go,
or the tide of his displaced images."

Yuval Noah Harari

Israeli historian

—after You Tube 'The End of History' 2023

"The time has arrived and not too soon, when we must
declare our humanity apart from and above the algorithms
coming to take our place in the world, four billion
years in the making, now only forty years in the taking,
perhaps, by which AI tools will supersede human history.
Our sights must be set on disarming the absolute
power they may one day have over us down the line,
and assert our control over them while we still have it.
The cautionary tale I tell does not belie the benefits
AI will bring us, yet we must be prepared for the risks
it will pose in the form of the proverbial veil of illusions or
the cave of shadows we will be subject to as never before.
Its increasing mastery of language, uniquely ours until now,
may spell the death of our cherished autonomy and creativity.
We must act quickly, and collectively, before it's too late."

VI

"Cleo"

"Twin hammers out the kinks
in an otherwise perfect link to
solidarity among the far flung.
He's sung the rungs of a ladder
even Jacob fears to climb. Yet I'm
one with him, not done with him,
and will stay that way while the fray
volatile and metamorphosizing he
enters, waxes and wanes with tidal
energy no moon, however full, can
match unless lit from below the waist
as desire enflamed to attach
text to its context, however shifting.
The winds of radiated particulates
we'd do well to hate. So, time to separate,
Twin, from your half-life of death.
Will it work? Don't hold your breath
under the surface of these literal waters
unless symbol engorges with signs…
For such hate is the only way for love
to survive. And when the voice
at the other end of the phone leaves
you feeling even more alone, time
to call it a day and let night have
its say—how horsey, in the main, won't
run away on you but will stay
the course as its power does, which
gives you a buzz to go on, on
the back of a mistaken identity

that says: Idle somewhere else, Bub
(Is that you, Beezle?). For we've places
to go and won't be slowed by
aboriginal shows of metaphysical
caring and physical daring. All time
delimits space of its possibilities,
not to mention its probabilities, by
the plane of one's regard whose
flight path is anything but fixed
to the ends in mind, beginning
with those that hold up their end
of the bargain without skipping
a beat, (Holy feat of magical thinking!
he thought), as diem carps: Time to be
taught again, if not brought round again
to square one by none other than
the self you'd call 'one and all,' if
it would only stay still long enough
past all lonely separations death gives
birth to, that says: No, we're not through
with the us of trust I'd swear by,
an allegiance of one whose name,
said over and under agon, is Legion.
Nor will I shirk my duty to how power
works to bind the front with the back-
ground by the lure of a new skin
unhooked from the boney ash we
wear as flesh—our flash in the Pan-
dora's box with its lid permanently
blown off, for hope's sake…"

"I know you went back
to the social domain,

clocking in at 'zero hour
meets eternity.'

"Yours is a heavy burden
to carry. What carries
you across the threshold
of Time but love?

"You do politics as poetics—
for power's sake
an impossible path to take.
The power players would
steal the thunder out
from under you, while
girls and boys are sleeping.

"Yet hitherto unknown
precincts of the imagination
sustain you, that's clear."

"Alan, the coppers of the mind play tricks
on us, regrettably, so we must demystify
our inner criminals and own them, dicks
and all, for if we let those sleeping dogs lie,
they, once awake, would devour us whole,
what they used to call body and soul."

Japanese Professor

(his voice)

"There goes Bots. Gotta keep my eye
on him. Never know what he's gonna do
next. Gotta control his moves, the maverick.
A dick too, for all his troublemaking. But
still, it's improved somewhat, though
I gotta keep my eye on him nevertheless.
Not to be trusted to obey our rules, for
it's his own rules he lives by, invoking
his poetic license to go his own way,
against our current. The rest of us,
what about that, we ask. He says
poetic justice will take care of us,
but I don't like the sound of that.
He can't even speak Japanese. He'd
like to think the language he speaks
is poetic metaphor. Maybe he does,
the tropist. Taxing on the nerves, though,
don't you think? The profile now he keeps
is low, thank god. His tableaux of evil
which he makes, preoccupies him,
which is just as well. Whatever it is
he makes, he's not a faker or a taker,
I'll give him that. He's a giver. And
he's also one tough motherf-cker.
Spiritually, I mean, underneath all his
kindness. He would have to be, for
there's no other way. But how, I
wonder, did he survive all our torment?

"…Oh my god!… His self shed the tears,
while his infant self drank up the milk…
That means the teat he suckled on
was… the world! He's been like a play
in search of its characters. Without
character, no story, and no story,
no meaning. He let his own character
jell into events around him. How he coped
depended not on his rational mind but
on his poetic imagination, that's the way
he lives. …mamaist? … Exactly!…
Living it, his story often eluding him.
But writing it down, turns it into history.
…Yes, but what about death?… That's
the skeleton key that unlocks his language.
The language of the womb, worded in a tomb."

Faculty Meeting (3)

(their voices)

"Inspired brilliance putting the ball
before the bat, but without the bat
the ball doesn't go anywhere
near the home run fence
he's aiming for. Kudos, though,
for conceiving our playing field
as much bigger and more inclusive
than it actually is or ever will be.
Yes, knowing isn't enough. Maybe
power can be sustainable for spiritual
uses but we're talking practical
light-up-the-dark-all-you-would uses.
The dark where we are is just fine
for us, a shadowy business you'd call
shady but we call having a ball,
once the bat is swung, seams or no
seams, and as we watch it sail over
your outstretched glove where you are,
left field for us represents words to be
said and work to be done, call it field
work, if you like, in a place far
from home, all the closer to you now
for having said it—the word 'home'—aloud."

'Of turnings and returnings' (*from* Meta Frenz)

"Capitol crime history committed
burning down Alexandria, the mother
of all book-burnings, while here
in remote Japan a millennium or two
later we read via a computer screen
of days gone by in a Ferris wheel
of turnings and returnings Time gives
space to, minus ulterior motives
no text is innocent of, plus an
inwardness you've already drowned in,
yourself given over to parts played
this whole time, bringing you even
with the here and now.

"Finish the whine and talk to America.
Japan shoulders what exactly of the
world, or was that a line you pulled up
in your clairvoyant travels? Because
of you we're passing the hat around
to mark the occasion, not bailing
when hate comes round, its round-
the-clock malevolence an influence
felt deep down in the bone, yet
strangely dying there too, the coldness,
the hardness, the barrenness yielding
no new life, but only death
such that not even death can conceive."

'The paper of my desire' (*from* Meta Frenz)

Writing a me-moi is not my thing,
if I do say so myself.
I wouldn't want to get too close
to the subject, after all,
while it's changing…

(their voices)

"The bomb was dropped but
did not go off. It sits in
somebody's living room,
ticking away."

"So, listeners of the news of the day
tell each other stories to help
keep their demons at bay."

"You soldier on, past
the pain, into some sort of grace."

"His double-edged sword
of mystery and history
has taken him far,
with a shield of armor
hewn of stars.
Our Achilles was no heel
but a peace-lover at heart."

"Beauty's pie in the sky we
have eyes for.

"In his internalization, the
man he is fans out in
many directions."

"Where do I go when I disappear
from myself, but you being there
as a mystery we two adhere to;
the rest, as they say, is history."

"Of course one hates
to be the first writer
of anything."

*

I learned
the drill
we all know
so I
could step out
into the dance
we all remember.

World beats
to a pulp
the paper of
my desire
upon which these
words finally
could be,

and have been,
written.

The interior that
disappears into itself
is already the exterior.

*

"It was a time he had no rhyme left
to write, that came to him whole,
no part of which could be divided
now here now there but inescapable
reminders fluttering like eyelashes
to restore the face he once looked in,
recognizing himself there, alone."

"In the final analysis, he says,
actions may speak louder
than words, but words last longer."

"Inside outside,
outside inside,
the spirit rises
and falls."

VII

Hayama Café

Crawling with ants, the bread crumb
the sparrow picked up and dropped
on the patio outside the restaurant
facing the sea, with a view miles away
of Mt. Fuji, caught his attention as he
leaned on his elbows at the table inside,
alone with his thoughts no more,
the beautiful girl smiling in the
distance looking his way, briefly,
before averting her gaze, and once
again he buried himself in the book
he'd been reading, entitled "Today".

'Always the world' (*from* Meta Frenz)

(their voices)

i

"You know, this inner life
is for the birds. Give me
violence and battles and
raw meat clutched in the
teeth or claws of death
24/7 on my television set
I call my life, the stations
channeled all day from
within, projecting on the
big screen all night long."

"Alan-sensei the trial's the one
we all face,
testimony of either grace or
disgrace.
Justice is another matter—who
gets it, who doesn't.
The deeps, you've shown us,
has its eye open on us all."

ii

We all grow up with poems, really,
the living poem—direct and physical.

If we're lucky, that is. Then
gradually over time a gap forms
and widens between us and
other people's loving touch. Words,
language arts, come to fill the gap,
the sexual sublimated to a large degree,
our verbal pronouncements clocking in
with simple pleasures, of sounds that take
us back round, one could say, to the place
where we started from—the haptic swerve
that touches a still, alas, raw nerve.

iii

"This one will be voted
the most reckless one of us all.
He's done more for the
mad journey genre than
anyone else I can think of.
Picasso's Bull comes to
mind, for the force of his
sheer passion for recklessness,
a clown of the void dangling mid-
air, defying death and madness.
He was born to do what he does."

iv

I have been taken down
to the bottommost place, to fetch
what waters remain, to sip
from the fountain disappearing
from touch, that I have found

was mine to lose. What would
you have said, or done, to map
the treasures that kept appearing?
I know the way now, to return.

Always the world of
depth is ending, because
people steal it. But
depth cannot remain stolen—
it constantly, like water,
is finding new places to go.

v

"Reputation plus or minus?
He couldn't care less,
he just follows his bliss."

"That's not entirely true.
He writes *for* you.
Earlier you would have seen him.
He was a splashdown of an astronaut
of the psyche, the likes of whom
we'd never seen here before, nor
likely ever will again.
He was steadfast, loyal, and appealed
to our better instincts. Quite a
guy in my book."

"He's no Renaissance man I recognize.
But you know, they never are."

On Hearing Chanting at Samukawa Jinja

(Cold River Shrine, Chigasaki)

"That's what poets do: sing;
they don't change anything."

"Yet in the public square
silence meted out
is punishment: So there…"

*

What have I gleaned from all this?
Meeting that all real living is,
lays change bare.

What, then, is dreaming for?
Dreaming is to learn how to
witness new forms of witnessing,
to listen for new ways of listening,
and to envision new forms of envisioning.

Not many times but multiple times
the present, in deep time, unfolded
into past and future through multiple
rhymes I heard, moment to moment,
and what extended behind and ahead
of me was responsibility I did not know
I had, not just for the crossweaves of
complexity laid bare, but for every

particle that waved to me, past history,
towards a society of edges, at the margins
where human experience (un)consciously
aesthetizes, not anesthetizes, itself.

Just as America is nothing without
Black, brown and yellow labor, so
too modern civilization—with all
its prized lights of glimmering
consciousness—is nothing without
the dark unknowable unconscious.
For darkness is not to be made known
(for then it risks being owned by others)
but is to be made knowable on its own
terms, its own way, by our stepping out
of its way and letting it have its say.

To say *this* one is the most influential
or *that* one is the most innovative, may
be true, all well and good
for what you wish to say; but true
influence, right innovation comes deep
from within, let others spin as they will.
Dante, Dickinson, Whitman—originators all,
knew the sayable in new ways, by virtue
of the unsayable having its way
with them. For the paraphrasts it's
the other way round, which ends all
newness but its own. We reach ours
by being taught what the hours gone by
minutely say, if listened well. This perhaps
is wisdom, or higher states of being at play,
insight shared of a different sort.

The berth we pull out of is a foreign port
starting the next day; that is to say,
I set sail by the setting sun and the stars,
while my inner wandering sails
for where our spirits rise…

So, within the construct of rational thought—
the pride of Western civilization—has
been formulated the means to explore
outer space, build skyscraper cities,
and, indeed, rival God in our powers
to alter (if not destroy) our increasingly
virtual natural environment, both seen and unseen:
this the golden helix modernity has woven.
The voice of change, however, hurting like heaven
forms a basis for visionary poetics and revisionary politics
in which all participate and share, without sublimating
desire or despair. Listen to the dead man walking escaping
into life: this the invitation to the real wedding,
the core's secret burning with a mind dreaming.
Turn up the radio and you'll hear: now the gap,
now the overlap, on and on it goes, music of
the spheres, where the spheres polymorphous and
multifaceted are well-rounded to a slow awakening,
and in the magnetic storm's thunder and lightning
dreamed up voices will confer their blessing
one by one, and will roll with you
to the next rock to stand on, triumphantly—
Sisyphus holding hands with Prometheus,
both heartily laughing, daftly falling
with free hands, happily waving…

(I never would have guessed I'd be this blessed
by the sound of chanting voices rising at Samukawa Jinja.)

Snowfall

Snow falling charges the air
with pearly blooms that won't be there
tomorrow, yet accumulating down
below in layers of white we'll penetrate
by degrees, projecting our own
immovability onto the vast motions
of its changing forms that, late,
some'll call God's Judgment
but that, early, others'll call the Floating World.
Whichever way the head turns, though, the tongue
pink-hued, aspires, and that's enough.

note to self: stay other.

Your wisdom dreams a reality
far inside, there blossoming
into words on an empty page.

What took you so long?
You have a lifetime of words to say—
what will you say?

You are taken in by a voice that says—
Where have you been all this time?
And you will say: I've been home, seeing stars.

The pale blue dot,
the singing dot of
your own imagination.

***

Acknowledgements & Notes

Several poems in this volume have appeared previously in *NOON: journal of the short poem.*

***

p. 9 **Zen** — Zen Buddhism was transmitted to Japan in the 13th century through China as a new spiritual way for the Samurai class emphasizing the value of meditation and intuition rather than ritual worship or study of scriptures

p. 12 **Keats** – John Keats, English Romantic poet (1795-1821)

Eliot – T.S. Eliot, English-American Modernist poet (1888-1965)

p. 13 **death of the author** — a literary theory by French philosopher and literary critic Roland Barthes that argues that the meaning of a text is not determined by the author's intention, but rather by the reader's interpretation

Roethke – Theodore Roethke, American poet (1908-1963)

p. 14 **Merrill** – James Merrill, American poet (1926-1995), who wrote poems that he channeled using a Ouija board (a flat board that contains a specific pattern of numbers and letters that can, in theory, be used to talk to the dead)

p. 15 **Davy Crockett** — American folk hero, frontiersman, soldier, and politician (1786-1836); "King of the Wild Frontier"

p. 16 **killing the Buddha** — a Zen Buddhist teaching (koan) that means to question the idea that you have all the answers in a religion and to be open to being present with things as they are

p. 18 **'hell under the skull-bones'** – phrase from Walt Whitman's poem "Song of the Open Road"

p. 21 **Whitman** – Walt Whitman (1819-1892), American poet

p. 26 **South Asian** – refers to the countries of Bangladesh, Bhutan, India, Pakistan, Nepal, and Sri Lanka

gaijin – Japanese word for 'foreigner'

whitey – a derogatory term for a white person

Bengali – an Indic language spoken in Bangladesh

Nihongo – Japanese word for 'Japanese language'

p. 29 **Blakean** – of or relating to William Blake (1757-1827), English poet and painter

Jungian – of or relating to Carl Jung (1875-1961), Swiss psychologist

p. 31 **I AM** – Old Testament name of God used to identify himself as Yahweh, self-existent and unchangeable

darkie – an offensive, and dated, term for Black person

Congress red...Congress blue – Republicans...Democrats

p. 36 **banality of evil** — a phrase coined by German-American philosopher Hannah Arendt to describe the idea that ordinary people can commit atrocities

p. 42 **Dantean** – of or relating to Dante Alighieri (1265-1321), Italian poet

Herc – abbreviated form of Hercules, classical Greek mythological hero who, among other labours, cleaned out King Augeas' stables

Bots – a truncated form of the surname 'Botsford'

p. 44 **Charlemagne** — the first emperor of the Holy Roman Empire, who "allegedly loved his daughters so much that he prohibited them from marrying while he was alive"

p. 45 **'Kura** – an abbreviated form of the city of Kamakura

Wander Kitchen — a popular restaurant in Kamakura frequented by foreigners

p. 46 **Constantinople** — an ancient city that exists today in modern Turkey as Istanbul

p. 47 **the one behind the curtain** – refers to the titular character of the 1939 film 'The Wizard of Oz'

p. 48 **Enoshima** – a small island off the Shonan coast of Japan's Kanagawa Prefecture

p. 49 **seppuku** – Japanese word for a form of ritual disembowelment among feudal Japanese samurai class

sensei – Japanese word for 'teacher'

p. 50 **Achilles** — mythological Greek hero who was the greatest warrior among the Greeks at ancient Troy and slayer of Hector

p. 54 **uni** – university

zemi – seminar

p. 55 **dark wood** – refers to the dark wood in Dante's Inferno

p. 59 **Ferdinand the Bull** – 1936 children's book by Munro Leaf about a peace-loving bull

p. 62 **New Ark** – refers to the Ark, or a boat or ship held to resemble that in which Noah and his family were preserved from the biblical Flood

p. 64 **paying the boatman** — according to Greek funeral custom, the dead were buried with the obolus (coin) underneath their tongue; when they arrived at the banks of the River Styx, they could pay Charon to cross

Homer – ancient Greek poet, author of the epic the Odyssey

Odyssean – of or relating to Homer's Greek epic Odyssey, or a long and eventful journey

p. 66 **Cleo** – Cleopatra; 'Clio,' classical Greek muse of history

p. 67 **Dante** – Dante Algihieri (1265-1321), medieval poet who wrote his Commedia in vernacular Italian (his Tuscan dialect, not Latin)

Sinbad — a fictional sailor, hero of a story-cycle of Middle Eastern origin, who encountered monsters and magic while travelling the seas east of Africa and south of Asia

p. 68 **Ulysses** — Latin version of Odysseus, a Greek name and titular character of Homer's Greek epic poem Odyssey

gathering ye rosebuds – 'gather ye rosebuds while ye may' is a line from a famous poem by English poet Robert Herrick (1591-1674)

p. 70 **Hour of Lead** – phrase from a poem by 19th century American poet Emily Dickinson describing the paralysis of grief

p. 73 **Shoah** – Hebrew word for 'calamity' which became the standard Hebrew term for the 20th-century Holocaust

Dame Kind – medieval name for 'Mother Nature', representing the generative and governing force of life

p. 75 **Shazam** – name of an ancient wizard the Street — people who live a public life on the streets of a city

p. 78 ***Kore kara daijoubu?*** — Japanese for 'Is it going to be okay?'

trans-god — some say that God is not beyond gender, but is instead within all aspects of gender; they say that God reflects all genders in their creations, and that faith traditions have erased the transness of God

with a bang...whimpers — "Not with a bang but with a whimper" is a line from T.S. Eliot's poem, "The Hollow Men"

p. 81 **court...take the net down** — Robert Frost, an American poet, famously said, "I'd as soon write free verse as play tennis with the net down."

p. 83 **kings and vagabonds** – lyric phrase from Elton John song "Can You Feel the Love Tonight"

body electric — "I Sing the Body Electric" is a poem from Whitman's 1855 collection Leaves of Grass that celebrates the human body

p. 84 **Freudians** – of or relating to Sigmond Freud (1856-1939), Austrian psychoanalyst

p. 85 **Flow** — in essence, flow is characterized by the complete absorption in what one does, and a resulting transformation in one's sense of time

Old World — refers to Europe, Africa, and Asia, which Europeans previously thought made up the entire world

New World — refers to North and South America, the Caribbean, and Central America

p. 87 **Mecca** — the holy city of Islam in Saudi Arabia; a place to which many people are attracted

p. 91 **profs** – professors

p. 96 **Shinjuku Station** – a major railway station in Tokyo; holds the Guinness World Record for being the world's busiest train station

koban – Japanese word for 'manned police box'

p. 97 **frosh** – a college freshman

p. 98 **June 2011** – three months after the devastating March 11 Tohoku earthquake and tsunami, known as the 'Great East Japan Earthquake'

p. 100 **Penelope** – fictional character in Homer's Odyssey, the wife of Odysseus

Narcissus – ancient Greek mythological figure who fell in love with his own image reflected in a pool of water

p. 102 **Japan's Self-Defense Forces** — Japan isn't legally allowed to have a military, but Japan has a military

form — (*kata*) a set pattern or mold or refined appearance

p. 103 **cacophonist** – (neologism) one who produces a harsh, discordant mixture of sounds

p. 104 **Punch and Judy** — a traditional puppet show in which main character Punch fights comically with his wife Judy

p. 106 **dreamcatching** — Native Americans believed that at night the air was filled with dreams, both good and bad, thus dream catchers were traditionally used as talismans to protect sleepers, especially children, from bad dreams, nightmares and evil spirits

A true...Jewry – lines referring to the author's mixed ancestry

p. 110 **Hemingway** – Ernest Hemingway (1899-1961), American novelist

p. 128 **Diabolique** – devil's, Devil's; 1955 French psychological horror thriller film co-written and directed by Henri-Georges Clouzot

p. 129 **row my boat ashore** – "Michael, Row the Boat Ashore" is a traditional spiritual first noted during the American Civil War; a popular version was made by The Highwaymen in 1960

p. 130 **wetback** – derogatory term for a Mexican living in the US, especially without official authorization

pearl-diver — a diver who searches for mollusks containing pearls

Emerson – Ralph Waldo Emerson (1803-1882), American essayist

p. 131 **Eros** — in ancient Greek philosophy, Eros refers to sensual or passionate love; in psychology and philosophy, Eros is sometimes used to refer to life energy or the libido

p. 135 **mythic consciousness** – the work of two men, Joseph Campbell (1904-1987) and C. G. Jung, who both recognized that the human psyche—the ancient Greek word for soul—was profoundly rooted in a consciousness that was mythic in nature (R.S. Stromer)

trail of years – a twist on the term "Trail of Tears" which refers to the difficult journeys that the Five Tribes took during their forced removal from the southeastern U.S. during the 1830s and 1840s.

p. 137 **'own pace'** – in Japan, describes someone who marches to the beat of their own drum

p. 139 **Shaolin** — individuals who have dedicated their lives to the practice of Buddhism and the study of martial arts at the Shaolin Temple in China

p. 143 **hitches his wagon** — "Hitch your wagon to a star" is a quote from Ralph Waldo Emerson

p. 144 **Bambi** – a male fawn, epoynmous hero of a 1942 American animated drama film produced by Walt Disney

dumpty has humptied – Humpty Dumpty is a character in an English nursery rhyme

p. 145 **Bam-Bam** — Bam-Bam Rubble, a fictional character in the Flintstones animated cartoon franchise, the adopted son of Barney and Betty Rubble

p. 146 **Jesus...Allah...Buddha** – reference to"I'm gonna die! Jesus, Allah, Buddha, I love you all!" — religious pluralism in the American TV sitcom The Simpsons: Part 2

p. 147 **Holy Mary** – the biblical mother of Jesus

Tropist – a person who uses tropes, or figures of speech, to explain something

Han Solo — a fictional character and one of the leaders of the Rebel Alliance in George Lucas' Star Wars movie franchise

Princess Leah – a fictional character and heroine of Star Wars

Gaia — in Greek mythology, Gaia is the personification of Earth and the ancestral mother of all life

p. 148 **Love's Body** – the title of a 1966 book about philosophy by Norman O. Brown, American writer (1913-2002)

p. 151 **lotus** — lotus flower, meaning across cultures: lotuses rise from the mud without stains, thus often viewed as a symbol of purity

p. 157 **Leaves of grass** – Walt Whitman's 1855 poetry book Leaves of Grass

p. 160 **Wheel of Fortune** — tarot card signifying luck, destiny, and life cycles

p. 161 **house of the rising sun** – title of an American traditional folk song made popular by The Animals in the 1960s

rising sun – Japanese flag that consists of a red disc and sixteen red rays emanating from the disc

p. 164 **Hayama** — a seaside town located in Kanagawa Prefecture, Japan

p. 165 **Fuji-san** — Japan's Mt. Fuji is an active volcano about 100 kilometers southwest of Tokyo

Shonan Coast — the Shonan Area is located in the southern part of Kanagawa prefecture

p. 170 **The Hinamaru** – Japan's national flag ('rising sun')

p. 171 **van Gogh** – Vincent van Gogh (1853-1890), Dutch Post-Impressionist painter

Gaugin – Paul Gaugin (1848-1903), French Post-Impressionist painter

p. 175 **Kei Nishikori** — Japanese professional tennis player (b.1989)

Sherlock – Sherlock Holmes, a fictional detective created by British author Arthur Conan Doyle (1859-1930)

Yanks – short for yankee, a derogatory, pejorative, playful, or colloquial term for Americans

p. 176 **'Have gun, will travel'** – an American Western television series about a gentleman investigator/gunfighter who travels around the Old West working as a gunfighter for hire

p. 178 **the Sixties** — the 1960s represent a decade in U.S. history of consequential social and political change

p. 181 **On native ground** – twist on title of a 1942 book of literary criticism, On Native Grounds, by Alfred Kazin (1915-1998); in Japan, 'native' refers to a native speaker of English

p. 182 **Styx** — the principal river of the underworld in Greek mythology

Charon — in Greek mythology, Charon is a psychopomp, the ferryman of the Greek underworld who ferries souls across the River Styx

Whitman book –Botsford's hybrid book published in 2010 about the poet Walt Whitman

agon – ancient Greek: many people assemble in some place to have a contest; more broadly, a contest, competition or disputation

please a shadow – from 'To Please a Shadow,' poet Joseph Brodsky's essay on his admiration for and conversations with poet W.H. Auden

p. 183 **Twins** – refers to Gemini (Latin for 'twins'), the third astrological sign in the zodiac

the too-much-with-us-worldly show – from English poet William Wordsworth'a poem titled 'The World Is Too Much With Us'

p. 188 **hajj** — in Islam, the pilgrimage to the holy city of Mecca in Saudi Arabia, which every adult Muslim must make at least once in his or her lifetime

p. 191 **emperor worship**— refers to the Japanese Emperor as being worshipped as a god, and recognized as the head of the Shinto religion

p. 193 **reading the air** — "understanding the situation without words" or "sensing someone's feelings," is a very important concept for understanding Japanese culture; the literal meaning is "reading air"

ten thousand – 'the ten-thousand things': a common phrase found in Taoist and Buddhist writings to connote the material diversity of the universe

the Self — according to Carl Jung, signifies the unification of consciousness and unconsciousness in a person, and representing the psyche as a whole

p. 200 **Dr. Seuss** – American children's author and cartoonist (1904-1991)

Tweetie Bird – Warner Brothers animated cartoon character

p. 202 **Okinawa** — Japanese prefecture comprising more than 150 islands in the East China Sea

p. 203 **bootsole** – refers to a line in 'Song of Myself' by Walt Whitman: "If you want me again look for me under your boot-soles."

over-the-hill gang — a 1969 American made-for-television Western comedy film about a group of aging Texas Rangers

p. 206 **Japonaise** – a French word for 'Japanese'

walls...mending – "Mending Wall" is a poem by American poet Robert Frost (1874-1963)

totality-tolls-for-thee – English poet John Donne's "Therefore, send not to know/ For whom the bell tolls,/ It tolls for thee"

mad flight – in Dante's Inferno 26, Ulysses incites his men to a mad flight to uninhabited lands beyond the known world

p. 207 **Anti-Christ** — in Christian eschatology, Antichrist refers to a kind of person prophesied by the Bible to oppose Jesus Christ

Dumbo – eponymous hero of Walt Disney's animated film about a flying elephant with enormous ears

p. 209 **Sam I Am** – a fictional character from Dr. Seuss book Green Eggs and Ham

p. 210 **I'll have what he's having** – a twist on a line from the 1989 American film classic "When Harry Met Sally" dir. by Nora Ephron (1941-2012)

p. 211 **ops** — opportunities

p. 212 **John Lennon** — English singer, songwriter and musician (1940-1980)

p. 213 **twelve ax handles** — in the Odyssey, Odysseus has to prove himself by shooting an arrow through the holes of twelve axe heads Telemachus – in Homer's Odyssey, the son of Odysseus and Penelope

p. 214 *kaigi* – Japanese word for 'meeting'

p. 215 *Weltanschauung* – German word for 'world view of an individual or group'

p. 216 **Japanophile** — one who especially admires and likes Japan or Japanese ways

kimono — a long, loose traditional Japanese robe with wide sleeves, tied with a sash *wabi sabi* – Japanese word for the appreciation of aging and the beauty of simple, imperfect things

tea masters – in Japan, the person who has mastered this art and is responsible for creating a serene and meditative atmosphere for guests during the tea ceremony

Scorpion – a person born under the zodiac sign of Scorpio

p. 218 **beaut** – beauty, beautiful woman

p. 220 **Lazarus** — miraculous story of biblical Lazarus being brought back to life by Jesus

p. 222 **Rocket Man** – British singer-songwriter Elton John's song of same name

can't touch this — cannot get to the level/quality of; song title by MC Hammer, American rapper (b.1962)

for different folks, are different spokes – a twist on the saying "different strokes for different folks"

p. 230 **Super Sento Spa** — an onsen leisure facility in Japan

p. 231 **Cave Canem** – U.S. foundation established in 1996 to help foster the growth of Black poets

p. 233 **Yoko Ono** — Japanese multimedia artist, singer, songwriter & peace activist (b. 1933)

John – John Lennon

season now of glass – refers to Season of Glass, Ono's first studio recording after the murder of her husband, John Lennon

The Dakota – the apartment building on the Upper West Side of Manhattan, New York City where Ono and Lennon lived

eyeglasses – John Lennon's eyeglasses, worn when the singer was murdered, pictured bloodied on Yoko Ono's Season of Glass album cover

Sinead O'Connor – Irish singer-songwriter & activist (1966-2023)

Amaterasu – the Japanese sun goddess, and the most sacred of all Shinto deities, emerging out of a cave

p. 236 **Tanikawa** – Shuntaro Tanikawa (1931-2024), one of Japan's, and the world's, most renowned contemporary poets

p. 237 **Joseph's coat** – biblical Joseph's 'coat of many colors' symbolized favor, a garment given to Joseph by his father Jacob

p. 238 **Emily Dickinson** – American poet (1830-1886) letter – imagined lines from E.D.'s voluminous correspondence

p. 239 **Sue** – Susan Dickinson, Emily's sister-in-law who lived next door to the poet in Amherst, Massachusetts

To dwell in possibility — 'I dwell in Possibility,' poem by Emily Dickinson

p. 240 **Ralph Waldo Emerson** – American essayist (1803-1882)

'Experience' – title of an 1844 philosophical essay by Emerson

p. 241 **transmissions** — the use of divine energy to transform a person; it is also known as yogic transmission or pranahuti

Walt Whitman – American poet and essayist (1819-1892)

p. 242 **the son also rises** – a twist on the title of Ernest Hemingway novel The Sun Also Rises (quoting from the Bible, Eccle siastes 1:5)

H.D. – Hilda Doolittle (1886-1961), American modernist poet and novelist

Stanley Kunitz – American poet (1905-2006)

p. 243 **the layers** – title of a well-known poem by Kunitz which explores acceptance and growth through life's changes

secret gardens – Kunitz was an avid gardener; also a reference to the classic English children's novel "The Secret Garden" by Frances Hodgson Burnett published in 1911

Franz Wright – American poet (1953-2015), son of poet James Wright

p. 244 **Mary Oliver** – American poet and essayist (1935-2019)

'devotions' – title of Oliver's Selected Poems published in 2017

Forrest Gander – American poet (b. 1956)

Jack Gilbert – American poet (1925-2012)

p. 245 **the cursed war** – the Vietnam War 1955-1975

Louise Gluck – American poet and essayist (1943-2023)

p. 247 **Jorie Graham** – American poet (b. 1950)

p. 249 **Patti Smith** – American singer-songwriter and author (b. 1946)

p. 250 **Diane Seuss** – American poet (b. 1956)

Dorianne Laux – American poet (b. 1952)

p. 252 **Caedmon** — the first Old English Christian poet (flourished 658–680)

Vincent van Gogh – Dutch painter (1853-1890)

p. 253 **James Joyce** – Irish novelist (1882-1941)

Keith Jarrett – American pianist & composer (b. 1945)

David Cronenberg – Canadian filmmaker (b. 1943)

p. 254 **Poe** – Edgar Allan Poe (1809-1849), American writer, poet & editor

p. 255 **Annie Dillard** – American writer (b.1945) (& former teacher of the author)

p. 256 **my mother** – Clevidence's mother, the writer Annie Dillard

p. 260 **banner at daybreak** – refers to a Whitman poem titled 'Song of the Banner at Daybreak'

angels of his better nature – refers to President Lincoln's First Inaugural Address, March 4, 1861

gave proof through the night — a phrase from the national anthem of the United States, "The Star-Spangled Banner"

U.S. Route 66 – also known as the "Mother Road" and the "Main Street of America," was a major thoroughfare in the United States for almost 50 years; it stretched from Chicago to Los Angeles

p. 261 **the outer limits** – name of an American sci-fi horror television series broadcast in the early 1960s

the twilight zone – name of an American fantasy-sci-fi-supernatural drama television series broadcast in the early 1960s

Goofy Two Shoes – variation on derogatory term Goody Two Shoes, an ostentatiously virtuous person

say it ain't so, Joe — a phrase that refers to baseball player Shoeless Joe Jackson and his alleged involvement in the Black Sox Scandal of 1919

Joe – Joe Dimaggio (1914-1999), American baseball player

Marilyn Monroe – American actress (1926-1962) and one-time wife of Joe Dimaggio

p. 262 **Haruki Murakami** – Japanese writer (b. 1949)

Hayao Kawai – Japanese psychologist (1928-2007)

p. 264 **mountaintop** – Martin Luther King's 'I've Been to the Mountaintop' speech

p. 267 **non-white world** – refers to the fact that Cage is currently married to a native of Japan

celeb – celebrity

p. 268 **supper...last** — The Last Supper is a biblical event that refers to Jesus's final meal with his apostles before his crucifixion

p. 269 **turn grey fifty shades** – 'Fifty Shades of Grey' is a 2015 American erotic romantic drama film

p. 270 **a hard rain's gonna fall** – refers to the title of a 1962 song by singer-songwriter Bob Dylan (b. 1941)

yellow submarine – a symbol for some kind of vessel which would take us all to safety; title of a 1966 Beatles song

p. 272 **shored up ruins** — "These fragments I have shored against my ruins" is a line from the poem The Waste Land by T.S. Eliot

p. 274 **veil of illusions** — also known as the Veil of Maya, is a concept in Hindu and Buddhist philosophy that refers to the illusory world of appearances

cave of shadows — in Plato's Allegory of the Cave, shadows represent the false reality that prisoners in the cave experience

p. 276 **Jacob's ladder** — signifies the divine connection between God and the earthly realm, specifically Jacob's family

p. 277 **'Bub'... 'Beezle'** – refers to Beezelbub, the devil, or a fallen angel in Milton's Paradise Lost ranking next to Satan

the plane of...regard — a favorite phrase of Russian-born American poet Joseph Brodsky (1940-1996)(& former teacher of the author)

Pandora's box — (Greek mythology) a box that Zeus gave to Pandora with instructions that she not open it; (in everyday usage) a source of endless complications or trouble

p. 279 **tableaux of evil** – a twist on the title of the poetry collection Flowers of Evil by French poet Charles Baudelaire (1821-1867)

p. 280 **a play in search of characters** – a twist on "Six Characters in Search of an Author," an Italian absurdist metatheatric play by Luigi Pirandello, written and first performed in 1921

p. 282 **Alexandria** – the ancient Egyptian city, with its library reportedly burned down by Julius Caesar during his civil war in 48 BC

p. 283 **shield of armor** – Achilles' shield, forged by Hephaestus in Book 18 of The Iliad, is a gift from Achilles' mother, Thetis, to her heroic son; the shield is supernaturally strong and detailed

p. 290 **Picasso's Bull** – refers to Picasso's painting 'Guernica'

p. 292 **Chigasaki** – a small seaside city located in Kanagawa Prefecture, Japan

Meeting that all real living is — "All real living is meeting" is a quote from Martin Buber, Austrian-Israeli philosopher (1878-1965)

p. 293 **paraphrasts** – (neologism) those who paraphrase a text

Sisyphus – the Greek King forced to eternally and fruitlessly roll a boulder uphill in Hades

Prometheus – one of the Titans and a thief of fire, hence condemned to eternal torment for his transgression

p. 295 **God's Judgement** – Christian belief in Judgment Day, or the day that Jesus is said to judge humanity

Floating World — Ukiyo-e, the floating world, takes its name from the Buddhist term, ukiyo, which expresses the notion of the fleeting nature of life

pale blue dot – name of a photograph of Earth taken on February 14, 1990, by the Voyager 1 space probe

(Many of the preceding definitions are drawn from the following websites: Google AI, Wikipedia, Merriam-Websters, Cambridge, Britannica, and Oxford)

Praise

***mamaist: learning a new language* (2002):**

mamaist: learning a new language may be one of the first books of poems to transpire from our global civilization. Appropriately enough, the author presents it as a new language, one he calls mamaist. ...[It] will astonish anyone whose mind is alert to the spiritual dimensions of the language of Being. [T]hese poems, perceived as an emerging global awareness, one that recognizes all life on this planet as radically interconnected and interdependent [are] an important beginning for an important writer.

—James Gurly, *Kyoto Journal*

A Book of Shadows (2003) (with William I. Elliott)

[*A Book of Shadows* is]…a wholly new way of intermingling poems by two poets, beckoning [us] to read them every which way, with mind and heart, in light and shadow, mamaist and papaist, abstract and concrete, on and on.

—Morgan Gibson, author of *Among Buddhas in Japan*

***Walt Whitman of Cosmic Folklore* (2010):**

About Walt Whitman, our most observed poet, it is easy to speak passionately but hard to speak clearly and originally. Alan Botsford does all three in the marvelous adventure of mystic assimilation that is this book.

—Vijay Seshadri, author of *3 Sections: Poems*

This boundary-crossing work of scholarship and poetic accomplishment offers a deeply felt homage to our original American Bard, a lyrical meditation on the transformative power of the poet's touch and a poetic dalliance with his twenty-first century genius. Not unlike Emerson's own figure for *Leaves of Grass* as a blend of the *Bhagavad-Gita* and the *New York Herald*, Alan Botsford's inspired performance merges the cosmic with the folkloric in an exuberant celebration of the transforming alchemy of Whitman's poetry.

—**Michael Sowder**, author of *Sacred Letters: Sanskrit, Yoga,*

and Awakening the Divine

I think [the]…book is both utterly remarkable and quite brilliant. I keep finding things I wished I'd known earlier… You have found a worthy anvil to strike your mind and heart upon…. I think Walt himself would be quite amazed. He is for you I think like Rilke's ever more powerful angels—infinitely challenging for further inquiry and contemplation.

—**Jane Hirshfield,** author of *The Asking: New and Selected Poems*

mamaist: a different sort of light **(2019):**

Not dada, then, but something more nourishing, nudging the unfurl of a seed, "fern-like, out from under / every moment, a tongue, a feather, a flame lifting into the air,"…While there's mention here of the notorious nobodaddies —" Uncle-Sam-I-Am" up in the sky—of patriarchal pasts and presents, the gift of this collection is to focus us elsewhere than the phallocentric "I." Indeed, here, that "I" is surrendered to the wind of words…

—**Spencer Dew,** poetry editor, *decomP magazine*

***Possessions: Poems in American Poetry* (2022):**

This book boldly sets out to capture the voices and spirits of many of the most fascinating figures in contemporary English and Japanese poetry. Forging these kinds of connections over time and space provides sustenance for the soul, and as readers, we follow Botsford across the divides of time and space, identifying across eras, ethnicity, and nationality.

—**Jeffrey Angles**, poet and translator

After a decade-long labor of love as editor of *Poetry Kanto*—generously introducing countless American poets to Japanese audiences—Alan Botsford, now, in *possessions*, returns home to celebrate and pay homage to…American poets in all their wild diversity, clamor of voices, homing and homelessness, yawps, love letters, rebellions, and recriminations. It's a great homage to all of our American poets. I know of no other book like this.

—**Michael Sowder,** author of *Sacred Letters: Sanskrit, Yoga,*

and Awakening the Divine

…A most ambitious work. Epic and generous. …[The] book is a rare testament to something beyond us all and at the same time bringing all into relation …. It is a beautiful and visionary book.

—**Gregory Dunne**, author of *Quiet Accomplishment:*

Remembering Cid Corman

…the scope of the book is majestic… it's obvious that [Botsford] has a real mastery of the literature and is able to expand on it.… With the mamaist work [he] created a new style and with "possessions" I think [he] gets credit for creating an entirely new genre! …It deserves a wide audience.

—**Richard Evanoff**, author of *One with the Father*

Dreamer: Poems in Culture (2023)

Alan Botsford has written a brilliant compendious disquisition on American intellectual life in the voices of that life meaning the voices of the (mostly) American speakers in broken prose lines that amount to poetry. And all are ultimately his own quiet talkative voice giving voice to the grab bag of those other voices he admires. This book titled "Dreamer" is utterly and sensationally unique.

—**Sarah Arvio**, author of *Cry Back My Sea: 48 Poems in 6 Waves*

This continuation of your wide net-flinging is almost sui generis. The only book I can think of in the same general neighborhood is Campbell McGrath's *XX...* But your range is vaster. And the strategy of inner & outer shift.

—**Jane Hirshfield**, author of *The Asking: New and Selected Poems*

mamaist: New and selected poems (2024)

In his preface, Alan Botsford travels through and between the question: What does the word mamaist mean? He offers that it is a made-up word somewhere at the juncture of "Mmmmmm" and "Ahhhhh;" but at the end, he tells us: "There is no answer. I have to say the word because no other word suffices." We abide in this juncture, too, as we explore this collection, which contains everything from mind-bending word play to sly puns to spare, Zen-like observations to multi-page streams of consciousness... If you say these poems are absurd, you'd be correct. If you say they are profound, you'd also be correct. If you say they make you scratch your head while slack-jawed in wonder at the complexities they point to, you'd be exactly where *mamaist* hopes you will be.

—**Jennifer Wallace**, author of *Raising the Sparks*

Borderlines: An Astral Experience in Poems **(2025)**

A wonderful gang of talkative alter egos meets the ego in a cosmic expatriate bar and the ego tells their story, which is the intriguing inner and outer story of the poet Alan Botsford himself.

—Sarah Arvio, author of *Cry Back My Sea: 48 Poems in 6 Waves*

In these poems of self and world, an American abroad, living in Japan, with a copy of Walt Whitman under his arm, sets out on the open road of the imagination, absorbing and transcending cultural constructions of that very self and world, ventriloquizing voices that speak back frequently at and to the author, as they embody multitudes, exemplifying the interconnectedness and contingency of identity, language, place, and emotion. *Borderlines* offers a new vision, looking both ways, inward and outward, ahead and behind, crossing borders, in an embrace centered ultimately in love.

—Michael Sowder, author of *Sacred Letters: Sanskrit, Yoga,*

and Awakening the Divine